PRAI[illegible]

"CX is a big business buzzword, but it needed Sunny to unpack it. Sage that he is, he blends stories and teachings in his usual concise, punchy, and digestible style. A truly enjoyable read."

—Kihara Maina, Regional Chief Executive Officer, I&M Group PLC

"Leading M-Pesa, I am constantly reminded that customer experience is not just about the products and services we build or the technology we deploy, it is about how people feel when they engage with us. That feeling is shaped, more than anything, by our culture—and that starts from the top. Sunny's book will give you both the spark and the structure to make CX real for you."

—Esther Waititu, Chief Financial Services Officer, Safaricom

"Nobody imparts knowledge and guidance drawn from their own personal experience in a clearer, simpler, brighter, more relevant, or more enlightening way than Sunny Bindra. *The X in CX* is quite simply a must-read for anyone wanting to take the customer experience within their business to the next level."

—Philip Coulson, Cofounder and Partner, Coulson Harney LLP, Bowmans Kenya

"Sunny's love for quality CX is shown in his argument that it only works if it's baked into the culture, shaped by leaders, and felt by customers at every touchpoint. What runs through this book is not theory but a fierce belief that customers deserve better—and businesses can deliver it."

—Kellen Kariuki, Chair, Standard Chartered Bank Kenya

"Sunny has a rare knack for cutting through clutter and complexity to reveal what truly matters. In a world hooked on overthinking, he delivers simple, sharp advice that actually works."

—Kush Bhardwaj, Executive Chairman, Optica Limited

X

Sunny Bindra

The X in CX

How to Deliver Customer Experience That Sticks

SUNWORDS LIMITED

Some names and identifying details have been changed to protect the privacy of individuals.

Published by Sunwords Limited, Nairobi, Kenya
https://sunwords.com/

Edited and designed by Girl Friday Productions
www.girlfridayproductions.com

Cover design: Paul Barrett
Project management: Abi Pollokoff
Editorial production: Kylee Hayes
Image credits: johnjohnson13/Shutterstock (speckle texture)

ISBN (paperback): 978-9914-37-446-9
ISBN (ebook): 978-9914-37-447-6

First edition

Dedicated to Team Sunwords

CONTENTS

1
It's the Customer, Stupid

There is only one boss. The customer. And he can fire everybody in the company from the chairman on down, simply by spending his money somewhere else.

—Sam Walton

Once a business is up and running, most of those involved in it just extract from it, every day.

The employees take out their salaries.

The shareholders take out their dividends.

The suppliers take out their dues.

> The government takes out its taxes.
>
> Which is the only group that puts money in, every day?
>
> You know the answer—that's why you picked up this book.
>
> It's the customer, stupid.

That seems like such an obvious thing, but it's easily forgotten. Only the customer puts money on the table every day; the rest just line up to take it out. The customer literally pays for everything. If you're involved in the business—as an investor, employee, vendor, or tax collector—everything in your life is paid for by customers. Your home, the food on your table, the car in your garage, the fees paid to your children's school.

The customer is the foundational provider for every other stakeholder in a business ecosystem. Ultimately, the financial sustenance that reaches all stakeholders flows from customers' wallets.

I am an advisor and educator working with corporations large and small, and I am acutely aware that my professional fees—and therefore all the costs of my life—are paid for not by my customers, but my customers' customers. It is therefore very much in my interest to be interested in the customer experience my clients provide.

Terms like *revenue* or *turnover* in our income statements disguise the essence: that customers willingly hand over part of their hard-earned incomes to buy our products or services. What they give us becomes our top line, the revenue line. That top line is the key line. After that line, all the extraction begins. When the top line is weak, the entire business shudders.

For the top line to be strong and steady, we need customers to be happy with our offerings. We need them to keep coming back. We need them to tell others.

Customers are central to an organization's *business strategy.* If customers are not the central pillar of the strategy, then something has gone very wrong.

Customers feature fundamentally in the organization's *financial plan.* Where else do revenues and profit margins come from, if not from happy repeat customers?

Customers are prominent in the company's *HR function*—because every employee should be involved in customer satisfaction, even those who never meet customers.

And customers are, in fact, the key component of the *brand* of the organization—because the best brand comes not from messaging but from the lived experiences of customers who buy your products and services.

Fundamentally, the point is this: Customers must *experience* us well—in every interaction, before *and* after they buy. *Customer experience* is the *CX* in this book's title.

Why do we emphasize customer *experience* these days, and not customer service or customer care or customer support?

That's because CX stems from the modern view

that our customers don't just feel us when they arrive to buy or use our offerings. They also experience us (or our lack) when considering their needs in life, and when looking for solutions to those needs. And, long after buying, we need to keep featuring in their minds in order to be considered afresh and seal their loyalty.

CX therefore captures the long journey customers have with a company. It encompasses every interaction at every touchpoint, from initial awareness and discovery to buying, using, and then contemplating the entire experience. Modern CX provides a much-needed holistic view of the manifold interactions our brands and businesses have with their customers.

Those interactions could take place in person, at our business premises. They could happen online or digitally, on our websites, apps, or social media platforms. They could take place with our humans, or with our bots and algorithms. They could even take place invisibly, in the minds of our customers! The point is, *all* the interactions matter.

Taking the broader CX view yields many benefits:

- It widens our focus and gives us many more areas in which to deliver great experiences.
- It is proactive and focused on the design of smooth customer journeys, rather than just responding to complaints and requests.
- It lifts us above mere transactions and pushes us to build lifelong relationships with customers.

- It works with a crucial truth, which is that customer experience isn't just what we think we offer; it's what *they feel* it is. As with all things human, feelings and perceptions rule. The art of CX is the art of managing emotional connections.

Nice. But wait—getting CX right, person after person, day after day? That's one of the hardest things in business.

WHEN EMOTIONS SPIKE

Fifteen years ago, my wife and I undertook a long flight with our very young son. It was a hot mess.

We checked in at our home airport just fine, and made it to the boarding gate with time to spare. But forty-five minutes to takeoff time, there was no sign of anyone opening the gate to the aircraft. Indeed, there was no aircraft in sight. Lots of passengers became irate and asked the only airline representative in sight what the problem was. He kept disappearing, presumably to ask his seniors hidden in the background.

He reemerged *after* the scheduled takeoff time to announce that the flight was delayed (duh) due to "operational reasons" (double duh) and that he could not provide a new takeoff time at the present moment (seriously).

The passengers, many like us with toddlers in tow, fidgeted on the uncomfortable metal gate-area seats for what seemed like an endless wait. The only concession made by the airline was allowing one person per family back out of the security gate to buy bottles of water from the duty-free shops. For most of the holdup, airline reps were in hiding behind closed doors, fearing the heat that would no doubt come from angry parents.

Long story short: We took off a full five hours later. Hungry, angry, defeated.

During the flight, I reflected on the many things the airline could have done differently. It could have warned us ahead of time, so that we could arrive at the airport later. It could have warned us at check-in and given us free entry to lounges to ease the wait. It could have stationed its people where we were to provide sincere apologies, concern, and help.

It did none of that.

But wait, the story has a good ending.

When we finally arrived at our destination hotel in the early hours of the morning, bedraggled and with sleeping infant in our arms, guess what? A smartly dressed hostess was waiting for us as we exited our transfer vehicle. The hotel had been tracking our flight and seen the huge delay. They knew we had a young child with us. So, the very concerned lady told us, she would just take our passports and skip check-in. Oh, and they had upgraded us to a suite to take the edge off our ordeal. We could go straight to bed and have a late breakfast, after which other details could be completed.

Wow.

I didn't get any sleep, but for a good reason! I lay in bed reflecting on everything the hotel had gotten right in CX. Genuine concern for their guests. Willingness to reduce frictions and spend some money in order to go the extra mile. Smart, empowered people at the front line to handle difficult situations.

And all that to remedy a situation that wasn't even their fault!

That, folks, is the *X* in *CX*—the X factor that helps some organizations get it so right. And that's what the rest of this book is about. What do these people know that most of us don't?

My emotions spiked twice that day. First, because of the airline—and my family hasn't used it again when we can help it. Second, because of the hotel—and we would book that hotel again, no questions asked.

Those emotional highs and lows come from moments of truth in the customer journey—the points at which the reality of the experience on offer is confirmed. In those moments, customers see you for what you are: incompetent or uncaring, as in the case of the airline, or as masters of the *X* in *CX*, like that hotel group was.

THE *X* IN *CX*

Let's start with a big reveal. What is the *X* in *CX*? What does it take to consistently deliver a very high standard of customer experience?

Does the secret lie in having good systems? Those

are vital, yes, but they aren't enough. Many corporations have very expensive, very capable systems—but still manage to piss customers off every day.

Is it to do with talent? Yes, very skilled, empathetic people are needed to deliver remarkable CX. But all the talent in the world is of no use if it doesn't gel in pursuit of a shared ideal.

Does the answer lie in just having great products—well-designed offerings that just do the job they are supposed to? Indeed, if your product is crap, you will not succeed in tricking people about it for very long. But even a great product is not enough by itself. For as long as you are selling to human beings, you will need to sell that product with smiles and goodwill.

If it was all just about systems, products, and people, many businesses would be masters of CX. But hardly any are. Or, when was the last time you had a standout experience as a customer?

Let's go back to my hotel, the one that wowed my family back then.

> It was a good hotel—good location, good food, good rooms. Product box ticked ☑.
>
> It had good people everywhere—refined, skilled. Talent box ticked ☑.
>
> It had good systems—remember how they could track our plane, and circumvent the usual check-in processes when necessary? Systems box ticked ☑.

That stuff is difficult enough, folks. It costs a lot of money and requires massive effort just to get those three boxes ticked. But it still isn't enough to be a CX master.

I spent the next forty-eight hours at that hotel, and there was more going on. I was very keen to figure out the X factor, and two days later I think I cracked it. Here's what I saw, starting with what I didn't see. The hostess who received us so expertly? We never came across her again! But her work was seamlessly picked up by others, equally friendly and attentive. That happened wherever we went in the hotel: The staff were invariably enthusiastic about being helpful. The first person we encountered wasn't a standout talent—she was just one member of a standout team.

So what does it take to make a group of people ready and willing to do the same thing at the same standard, day after day? You know the answer as well as I do.

It takes a *culture*.

That thought has been reinforced for me, uncountable customer experiences later. When CX is really bad? It's the culture. When it's surprisingly good? It's the culture.

Culture, in this sense, refers to how a group thinks and responds to shared challenges. For a business, caring for its customers is one of the biggest challenges going. Whether it will pull this off depends wholeheartedly on how its people behave, day after day.

Do the people actually care about caring for customers? Or, as in most organizations, do they just pretend they do? Do the people have high standards in dealing with customers? Are those standards rewarded and appreciated? Are lapses viewed with serious concern?

Culture comes from how much people care, and how seriously they regard their work. When culture is strong, it leads to a set of daily habits—habits that are sacred, habits that are followed day after day.

The *X* in *CX* is hidden in culture—and daily habits.

This book is about where that culture comes from in the first place.

CX masters know how to pull off regular, consistent CX, to a very high standard.

It's time for you to know what they know.

2

CX Is Broken

The lonely road to greatness is better than the crowded road to mediocrity.

—Matshona Dhliwayo

A customer walks into a brand-new mega-mall on a weekday. It boasts many household names in shopping, both local and global. It's virtually empty.

She enters an internationally renowned supermarket. Here, too, customers are thin on the ground. She's looking for a refrigerator—a sizable purchase—among other things. It's a huge store, so she asks for help. Few assistants seem to know where things are displayed. Not one offers to walk her to the correct area. Eventually she makes her own way to the right place.

She looks through the stock of fridges on display. Again, no assistant comes to help or to explain features or to, you know, *sell*. The customer makes her own decision and settles on a particular brand and model. She looks for an assistant to book the item. She is now told that the piece on display is the last one remaining. It is shopworn and shows wear and tear. Reluctant to pay for something less than pristine, she asks the assistant to check whether other branches of the store have this item in stock. She is told the branches all run "different systems" and she will have to go across town personally to check. The assistant does not even offer to call the other branch.

The truth is, we rarely have great customer experiences. Across all industries and sectors, we merely tolerate those we buy from.

Disappointed, the customer walks out and sees hope: An international electrical-goods producer has its own branded shop nearby. She peeks in and sees some refrigerators on display. This is a much smaller store, so she is hopeful the service will be a little better.

Nothing doing. The shop is devoid of customers, but not one employee looks up or comes over or offers to help. Our customer can't see anything she might buy. She walks out.

Later, at a small, local, family-run store where she hopes to find other products on her shopping list, she encounters one family member berating her employees in a high-decibel rant, accusing them of stupidity and laziness. Amid the shouting, neither shop owner nor staff members notice the customer. Our hardy shopper sees what she came for and goes to pay. At the till, another family member is engrossed in a personal phone call, headphones on, chatting away in full vernacular. She does not even make eye contact with the buyer, let alone crack a smile, while recording the sale.

I didn't make up those examples; they were recounted to me on the day they happened.

Many traditional shops, in malls or on main streets, are struggling. You would think that in difficult economic times a customer looking to make major purchases is especially valuable and will get exceptional, even excessive, attention. Not a bit of it. Most of our shops just don't get this thing called customer service. It doesn't seem to matter whether they are international brands or local, large stores or small, with the owner present or not. They are indifferent to customers. They don't value them. They don't even go the standard miles, let alone the extra one, to make a sale. Even during a shopping recession.

I hear these examples all the time, and I am always left perplexed. What part of this do shop owners, shopkeepers, and shop assistants fail to understand? The customer is everything. What you sell pays for it all: your rent, your salaries, your meals, your children's school fees. Why do you not care?

Or perhaps more accurately: Why has no one made you care?

Many big global names—Sears, Toys"R"Us, CVS, House of Fraser, Debenhams, Body Shop—have fallen out of popularity or are in distress in recent years. It is not a time for any retailer to be complacent. But isn't ignoring your customers the height of complacency?

We have some brilliant shops, of course we do. These stores are a pleasure to visit. The staff are full of smiles, the merchandise is intelligently chosen, and proper help is always at hand. We love those places and return often to them. But tell me, how many such stores can you name?

The truth is, we rarely have great customer experiences. Across all industries and sectors, we merely tolerate those we buy from.

THE MACHINE WILL SERVE YOU NOW

Personally, I love technology. I am delighted when things that used to take forever—like banking or food delivery—are done with just a few taps on a smartphone. I'm all for it.

A while back, the promise was this: CX will get way better once machines replace humans. It's humans who are lazy, ill-motivated, surly, and uncooperative.

Once we root them out and bring in hardware and software to do their work, customers will rejoice. Their experiences will become quicker and smoother.

So how's that worked out?

If you visit any major city post-pandemic, you will notice that low-touch automation is everywhere these days, cranked up to the max. Airports deploy self-check-in counters. Passport control is done via scanners. Supermarkets require you to check out your own groceries. Restaurant chains make you order using QR codes from your table. Banks hate it when you show up at a branch. Delivery apps try their damnedest to prevent you from talking to an actual human.

Humans, it seems, are in short supply. Even though there are well over eight billion of us on this planet.

What's really happened is that instead of improving CX, corporations are just cutting staff costs. Using machines isn't about making things better for customers; it's about shrinking payroll. Using the machine directly is rarely a better experience for the customer, but it is a far better one for the senior executive and the shareholder, at least in the short term. The cost of doing business goes down, and if you can maintain the top line, the bottom line looks much better. Champagne all around—for now.

The catch was hidden there in that last paragraph: *if you can maintain the top line.*

If you insist on degrading the customer experience, good luck in maintaining that top revenue line. For a while, we customers will put up with poorer service, because we are habit-bound creatures (more on that later in the book). But if the checkout scanners keep failing and we have to wait forever for a human to help us, blood pressures and temperatures will rise. Eventually, we will walk out and not come back. Your top line will crack.

This happened to me during a family trip to Milan, Italy, recently. We went into a clothing store, a well-known family brand. Each floor, weirdly, seemed to have one employee. Just one. Lots of snazzy tech, though. After choosing your items, you were required to throw them all into a checkout basket. The built-in tech was so good, it could read labels without anything needing to be held up to a scanner. *Nice,* I thought.

But wait. Every item of clothing had a security tag attached to it. Each one had to be removed; otherwise, it would trigger an alarm when taken out of the store. The scanner tried to show us a nice video on how tag removal should be done, but the procedure was intricate and not easy to do the first time you tried it.

So we had to search for the sole human. We found her in a corner, trying to put a bunch of tried-on clothes back on display. She put everything down to come and help us. I asked her if they were short-staffed that day. Were her colleagues off sick or something? No, this was normal. She was the only employee on that floor. It was her job to help people who asked questions, guide them to the changing rooms, refold or rehang the clothes they discarded, and help them check out when the fancy machine couldn't pull it off.

She looked bedraggled and frustrated, and I felt sorry for her. I hoped they paid her a lot to do the work of four people—but I bet they didn't.

I'm sure this made great sense to someone high up and far away. *Ooh, we can clock the same sales with a quarter of the staff we used to have! The new machines are great; they can do it all!* Turns out, no. On both counts. I will not be returning to that store.

Surveys show that a third of shoppers—especially Gen X and older—hate automated checkouts. Automation has led to a marked increase in shoplifting. Many shoppers resent being forced to do the work the retailer used to do. Some don't like the idea that the machines they are using put real humans out of jobs.

So is your cost saving actually real?

This is what happens when great CX is not central to your CEO's business strategy. This is what happens when your CFO never visits a branch or meets a customer. This is what happens when you pay millions to technology vendors and your branding agency, but peanuts to the humans who could be central to your CX offering.

GREAT CX IS STILL RARE

The first book I wrote was an angry one.

Crown Your Customer came from my own experiences of ridiculous customer treatment and from watching customers everywhere being treated like cattle. It was a call to arms to both the providers of customer care and their victims to put an end to the nonsense. Back then, standards were generally lamentably low. Customers were made to queue up, wait and wait and wait, get messed up or turned away, and generally treated with disdain.

I am a little less angry these days.

Partly, that's because a decade or two later, things are generally better. It doesn't always feel like it, but businesses understand the centrality of their customers a little more deeply now. They make more of an effort to be quicker, more helpful, and more caring. For example, the speed with which regular bank transactions can be conducted these days, using digital channels, is an order-of-magnitude higher. Many businesses now make it quicker and easier for us to deal with them. Most have learned to consider the totality of customer experience at all touchpoints to raise their game. Many have injected new technology to make things quicker and easier.

And yet we all sit up, surprised, when customer experience is good—because it's still usually a surprise.

I recently had one of those rare moments of good CX at a medical center. From the front door, things were different. The security guard jumped up to open the door with a smile. The receptionists were efficient and helpful, despite the crowd. Technology was smoothly in play—everything tracked and entered into the system.

I needed to move from room to room, but never was I just told where to go—someone came to get me and guide me. This interplay of human and machine made the whole thing work. A complicated people-movement process was done with minimal friction.

Was it perfect? Not at all. There were some glitches and delays; some people did not quite do what they were supposed to. The point is, by and large I was impressed and satisfied. Human errors occurred, as they always do, but there was rapid recovery and remediation. That's as good as it gets.

Great CX is still rare. What is surprisingly common is bad CX.

Looking back, there was nothing really *wow* going on there. That organization was behaving as all organizations should: making it easy for customers to deal with them, not wasting their customers' time, deploying technology intelligently, and throwing in a smile or two for good measure.

Why is that so hard to do?

Great CX is still rare. What is surprisingly common is bad CX. Even organizations whose customer-service excellence is generally appreciated and even praised can fall surprisingly short. In recent times, I have personally had the following experiences: A global e-commerce giant sent me damaged goods, then refused to make things right. An airline canceled a flight with forty-eight hours' notice, wrecking a family holiday, and then disappeared. A major retailer can't even maintain basic online communication.

Oh, and those folks who promise they'll "get back to you after checking"? They almost never do, so it's a genuine surprise if one actually does!

Many businesses still crawl at old-world response times, as if instant messaging never happened. It seems they are stuck in the world of carrier pigeons and messengers on horseback.

I am not referring to some small-time, small-town operators in my hood, please note. Some of those being surprisingly disappointing are global giants, behemoths in their industries, renowned (in the past, at least) for their CX dazzle. Others are well-regarded market leaders. They have the resources to fix this, but somehow choose not to. Many are folks I have done business with for decades. You'd think they wouldn't want to lose me as a customer, but here we are.

BAD CX IS YOUR SUICIDE NOTE

Over decades as a business advisor, I have heard a long litany of reasons given to me by CEOs explaining why their businesses are suffering.

> It's not us; it's the economy that keeps tanking because of bad policies and external shocks.

> It's not us; who could've predicted COVID-19?
>
> It's not us; it's the unfair competition we are subjected to.
>
> It's not us up here; it's the quality of staff down there.

Don't get me wrong: These challenges are real and often serious. But businesses are rarely killed from the outside. In my lifelong observation, the problems begin inside. It's leadership failures. Poor standards. Weak employee engagement and retention. Shaky working capital. Lack of rigorous routines. A workplace no one's proud of.

And then there is the focus of this book: bad customer experience. You can get away with that one for a while, folks, but keep doing it, and all you are doing is penning a long suicide note.

In Ernest Hemingway's famous novel *The Sun Also Rises*, a character is asked how he went bankrupt. "In two ways," he answers, "gradually and then suddenly."

That famous line sums up how businesses fail too. We notice only the sudden collapse—banks calling in loans, unpaid salaries, court cases—but the truth is, the cracks appeared long ago.

It all feels dramatic and sudden, and we look for answers in the here and now.

But those answers can only be found way back.

Most businesses that die are not killed suddenly;

they kill themselves—gradually, then suddenly. It is many years of neglect that explain the sudden ending.

Businesses die for a wide range of reasons. They fail to stay relevant to their customers. They indulge in various bad practices. They have weak governance and controls. They fall back in the race with competitors. They are unable to address disharmony in their key people. They borrow heavily on waves of unfounded optimism.

None of those pathogens arrive suddenly. They take time to manifest, weakening the organization slowly but surely. And so a failing business can look like it's succeeding for quite a while before it finally goes bust. The drama catches everyone's attention, but what should have been attended to happened slowly, over many years.

Bad CX is exactly like that. Because it's hard to do, we give up on it, bit by bit. We let the standards slip, inch by inch. Because customers don't flee at the first bad experience, we start taking them for granted. Bad CX is the slowest-acting pathogen.

But one day, customers will leave. In swarms. And by then, it'll be too late.

Ask Sears, whose long checkout lines in outdated stores heralded their eventual demise.

Ask Blockbuster, who could not see streaming video coming and persisted with the fading customer experience of physical movie rentals.

Ask BlackBerry, whose dominance in business smartphones made them arrogant enough to believe that a physical keyboard, a clunky operating system, and a lack of apps would not hurt them.

Bad CX is the suicide note you don't even know you're writing.

3

The *X* in *CX*

We are what we repeatedly do. Excellence, then, is not an act, but a habit.

—Will Durant

Customer Service Week is now a global phenomenon. Businesses everywhere take a moment to remember and appreciate their customers, with special events, colorful outfits, freebies, and social media buzz lighting up the week.

It's . . . nice. Kind of.

Here's the truth: People love events more than processes. Most folks enjoy having their birthday celebrated. It doesn't matter if they've done anything noteworthy all year—it's a special date and there's cake, so let's celebrate.

Corporate life is packed with what can seem like frivolous festivities, but they matter too. These events build camaraderie and create bonds, acting as the glue that holds together a business where rewards often skew toward a select few. People need to feel connected, and sometimes the only way to show that is through ritual celebration. Employees generally like events like Customer Service Week because it adds variety to their routine work lives.

Most customers appreciate the unexpected gift or attention—just like a birthday cake. It's charming, sort of.

But for those of us who aren't easily charmed by freebies and festivities, here's the problem: Since when did serving customers well one week a year become okay?

Smart business leaders see through this. Customer Service Week should add excitement, but it must come on top of consistent, year-round excellence—not as a substitute for it.

Too many businesses treat Customer Service Week like a quick fix—a shallow, low-effort substitute for daily excellence. It's easy to spend a budget for seven days; it's much harder to build a culture where staff instinctively give their best every day.

The real prize isn't winning Customer Service Week. It's delivering continuous customer excellence.

Every year, I get surprise gifts from service providers during Customer Service Week. I only appreciate them if they're *already* good at customer care. Greetings and offers from businesses known for bad service don't impress me. You can't fake great customer experience—it takes real work and leadership.

My wife has a suggestion for a great Customer Service Week idea: Reveal to your customers the top three most common complaints from the past year and the steps you're taking to fix them permanently. That's how you aim for everyday excellence.

Any takers? Didn't think so. Party on.

Businesses serious about CX know it's not a one-off event. It's a way of life—a habit.

Real success comes to those who make CX a daily habit. They don't need flashy celebrations because their offerings speak for themselves.

The *X* in *CX* is just that—your ability to turn great customer experience into a regular, repeated occurrence.

IT'S WHAT THEY FEEL

Before we go any further, let's clear up a common misconception.

As I wrote a little earlier: Great CX isn't about what you offer; it's about what your customers *feel.*

You might think you've set everything up perfectly—great people handling customers, top-notch systems, slick processes, solid product design. But none of that matters if your customers don't feel it.

Feelings drive everything. The most extraordinary human achievements come from stirring deep emotion in a group of people.

The best leaders have always known this. Nelson Mandela generated so much goodwill that the collective desire of millions got him out of prison—and into power. Barack Obama convinced a majority of American voters to go "against" their race and pulled off what seemed impossible. Wangari Maathai made people feel deeply about protecting the environment, in a society that had forgotten to care.

And it's not just the good guys who get it. Adolf Hitler played on his people's insecurities to spark a world war. Today, neo-fascists are all over the world, stoking those same fears. *Why am I poor? Whose fault is it?* Those feelings are weaponized to target minority groups—and often lead to landslide election wins.

Feelings drive everything. The most extraordinary human achievements come from stirring deep emotion in a group of people.

Effective leadership, whether for good or ill, hinges on the ability to understand, influence, and shape emotions.

History shows that all major collective achievements, in every culture, in times of war and peace, happen on a wave of emotion. When people act in unison, they're moved by sentiment, not spreadsheets.

Study humans, and you'll see we're not just mostly water—we're mostly feelings. Your favorite food brings comfort and nostalgia. A threat creates fear or loathing. Songs make us happy or sad. Betrayals ignite lifelong anger. We catch feelings from body language before a word is spoken. Everything is emotion.

Even if you get this, though, there's a catch: Managing feelings is no easy task.

Feelings are unpredictable and messy; they can't be measured. They grow fast and change faster. Trying to manage them flies in the face of traditional leadership training. Most of us are more comfortable with key performance indicators than emotions. We'd rather focus on sales, head count, and gross margins than the emotional climate of an organization.

In CX, your customers don't quantify your offering—they feel it. You might care about customer churn, complaint rates, or first-time resolution, but customers don't think in percentages. They just feel—and act on those feelings.

So let's start by understanding those feelings.

THE TEN CUSTOMER BUTTONS

You think you sell solutions and specifications? Nope.

People buy feelings, not products. So sell feelings!

Talk to customers, and observe them. What is your product generating—or failing to? Are the feelings of buying and using your product consistently positive or at best neutral? Are you, heaven forbid, sparking off negative feelings in your buyers on a regular basis?

Apple Inc. is the master of selling feelings. This company doesn't sell a spec or a functionality; it sells aspirations and ease and community—at premium prices.

What you call your customer experience is actually your customers' feelings about your offering. So let's see if we can categorize those feelings.

The diagram below shows the range of positive feelings generated in customers by business offerings. Which buttons are you pressing in your customers?

THE 10 CUSTOMER BUTTONS

VALUE This is a good deal	**UTILITY** This does what I want	**QUALITY** This is good stuff
CONVENIENCE They make it easy for me	**AFFINITY** I relate to these people	**RESPECT** I admire this organization
STATUS This reflects well on me	**AFFECTION** These are nice people	**SUCCESS** They'll make me a winner

Discount retailers go big on *value*. Their entire existence hinges on creating this particular feeling in customers: *This is the best deal I'll find; this will save me money.*

Mercedes, on the other hand, ignores the Value button and hits hard on Quality and Status. When customers sense Quality, it gives them trust, confidence, and the feeling that their money was well spent. Status? That's about signaling achievement or arrival—something that makes the buyer feel they've reached a higher plane.

Apple Inc. presses those same buttons, but with a heavy dose of Utility and Convenience. It's aspirational, a status symbol; yet Apple products are designed to be effortless. Tap a button and they just work—a powerful combo.

Safaricom's M-PESA? It pressed the heck out of the Convenience button. Suddenly, millions could transfer money in seconds by tapping their phones.

Equity Bank revolutionized mass banking in Kenya by hitting the Affinity button. It made customers—who had long been ignored by traditional banks—feel wanted, understood, and valued. The bank even called them "members," not customers. The result? They showed up in droves.

Let's make it personal. My own professional practice, which provides advisory services and executive training, is laser-focused on the Success button. My clients hire us for one reason: They want to feel that we're making them better and setting them up to win. You probably picked up this book for the same reason—to learn about CX so you can win more often.

The first four buttons—Value, Utility, Quality, and

Convenience—are the usual suspects. From Audi to Zoom, many brands play with them. But the next five—Affinity, Respect, Status, Affection, and Success—are trickier. They tap into deeper emotions, and it takes a true CX master to unlock them.

Let's take Affinity. Brands like Tusker beer, with its hundred-year legacy in East Africa, nail it by playing on patriotism and cultural pride. People buy because they feel they belong.

Then there's Respect—this one takes decades of consistent behavior to earn. Take Standard Chartered's "Here for Good" slogan, born out of the global financial crisis. When many competitors tainted themselves with shady practices, this slogan became a statement of ethics and long-term commitment. Powerful—but there's a catch. Respect isn't just a slogan; it must be earned every year.

Status, of course, is tied to cultural esteem. Germany's cars, Italy's fashion, France's cuisine—each purchase of those things comes with an implicit boost in social standing. But this only works when the status is easy to spot and universally recognized.

Success? That's a tough button to claim. Only a select group of advisors, coaches, and trainers can trigger that feeling. And it only works if the customer sees and feels real success later on in life as a result of your offering; otherwise, it fades away fast.

Finally, we come to the rarest of them all: the Affection button.

Here's a question: Is your business liked?

We don't often think of businesses in this way.

We're transactional—offering products or services, paying employees, returning profits to shareholders. Who needs to be liked?

But if you think like that, you're missing out—big-time. Being liked by employees, customers, investors, and partners is a huge advantage. Few pull it off, but the ones that do? They thrive.

Small local shops and service providers are great examples. They survived economic downturns, e-commerce, and the internet. Why? Because they have local knowledge, offer personalized service, and foster a sense of community. We like them because we feel connected, and we know our purchases support their families.

Big businesses struggle with this. When was the last time your bank or supermarket made you feel known? Do you ever visit a corporation just for a chat? Is dealing with a large corporation a joy in your life? Do you wish for the success of mega-corp shareholders? Unlikely.

So the real question for big businesses is: How can you be liked more? Being genuinely liked by customers creates the strongest bond of all.

And now, sharp-eyed readers may have noticed I promised ten buttons, but only mentioned nine. I saved the best for last.

The Wow button sits atop the rest. It gets pressed when you deliver genuine, positive surprises. That feeling of "I didn't expect that—they've gone above and beyond." That's magic. Wow moments spike positive emotions when we least expect them.

Wow can happen when a product turns out to be better than expected, or when customer service is unexpectedly brilliant. It can be in the form of compliments on something we bought, or just encountering staff who are way nicer than we anticipated.

A while back, my family stayed at the Raffles hotel in Singapore to see if its famed service lived up to the hype. Over breakfast, my young son was chatting about a soccer game he hoped to watch that night. The waiter, overhearing the conversation, discreetly checked with the entertainment team to see if the game would be shown. He returned with a note detailing the channel and time.

But it didn't end there. Later that evening, we returned to our room to find a handwritten note stuck to the TV, addressed to my son. It read: "I hope you had a lovely day. I've set the TV to the right channel for you, and left some snacks to enjoy during the game. Just switch it on at 9:00 p.m.!"

Wow. There's nothing quite like someone going out of their way for your child, right?

I wasn't watching much soccer that night. My mind was on something else: What does it take to build a culture where even the average employee goes the extra mile for customers, without being asked? How do you create an environment where delivering Wow is second nature? That's the *X* in *CX*, and the rest of this book will explore that.

Now, let's close on the ten customer buttons. You don't have to press all of them—it's impossible. The key is to own two, three, or four, and make them central to your CX strategy.

Take Microsoft, one of the world's most valuable companies. Its software and hardware are used by over 90 percent of global organizations. That's an enviable position, but it comes from owning key customer buttons for decades: Quality, Utility, and Respect. Its core products work, and they work well. Customers don't have to love Microsoft, but they respect it.

The lesson? Own your buttons and deliver on them—consistently. Just don't be so bad on the others that you create negative feelings.

One last note about the buttons: Don't base your entire CX strategy on the Wow button. It's costly, hard to replicate, and once you've wowed a customer, the next time they expect it as normal! For most organizations, making things effortless for customers should be the priority.

To understand that better, let's shift from customer buttons to customer journeys.

THE DESTINATION IS THE JOURNEY

Every day, we invite our customers to join us on a journey. They start somewhere, have some adventures along the way, and hopefully arrive at a place worth reaching. Then the journey begins again.

This is the modern framing of customer experience. It's a shift from viewing customer interactions as isolated touchpoints to seeing them as part of a continuous, holistic experience. It maps out the entire process customers go through when interacting with your company. Please note, though: This journey does not begin when the customer actually starts transacting with you, and it does not end when the transaction is complete. Modern thinking about customer journeys emphasizes this point: CX occurs long before customers interact with us formally and long after they are done with the transaction. Customer journeys stretch all the way from initial awareness to post-purchase engagement.

Most businesses focus only on the middle—when the customer is *buying* or *using* their product. They leave the other stages—like *preview* or *evaluation*—to the sales and marketing team.

That's a big mistake. Customers don't care about your internal departments; they see you as one brand, one experience. Viewing the customer journey holistically lets us see things from their perspective, not just our own.

So let's break it down from the customer's point of view, using the example of a family contemplating a home move.

Having decided to move and identified their new home, the family will wonder: Do we need a moving company? Will our furniture fit the new house? Should we buy a bigger refrigerator? How much work will the new place need? This is the stage at which needs are manifested or recognized.

One event triggers needs for multiple products and services. The customer then moves on to an evaluation stage, where they weigh their options.

Traditionally, these early stages have had little to do with customer-service teams—they're seen as being in the realm of strategy and marketing. That's wrong. Modern CX thinking understands that the journey begins in the customer's mind. Will your brand come to mind when they think "refrigerator"? Will your moving firm show up as a top option, recommended by others? Will they call your insurance company if they're worried about damage?

CX and marketing teams must work together, because customer perceptions form long before they ever step into your store or office. Will they find you easily? Will they hear good things about you? Will you be simple to contact? All of this matters.

If you're in the game from the start, the customer moves on to the acquisition stage—when they have decided to buy from you. How will that go? Will the experience be quick, clear, and easy? Or will you confuse them with too much information or make them wait because of your inefficiencies? How good is your website? Are your staff adept at closing the deal? Are customers helped—or hindered—when they want to hand you their money?

Let's assume you handled the sale well and the deal was closed. Next, the customer starts a utilization stage—they start using what they bought. Is your CX present here? Is your product easy to set up, or are they left to muddle through confusing instructions on their own?

CX is the whole shebang—from the first recognition of a need to the final follow-up message.

Quick aside: When I was a young professional in London, IKEA was the go-to for stylish, affordable furniture. But the flat-pack assembly? A total pain. We all kept going back to IKEA, though—they were still wiping the floor with traditional furniture stores. Fast-forward to the 2020s, and IKEA has evolved. Busy young families don't want to visit massive stores for small needs. So IKEA has invested in online shopping, smaller stores, home delivery—and even furniture assembly for an extra fee.

These guys get it: CX is the entire journey, and what worked in the past might not work today.

Using your product calls forth many emotions. A great product evinces joy; a bad one evokes feelings of disappointment, even anger. No amount of fancy selling can make up for a dismal user experience.

There's also a final stage in the journey. It involves contemplation of the whole experience. Here, the customer asks: So how did that go? Were these guys helpful? Did they drop the ball once I paid? Is this product reliable? Would I buy from them again?

That, then, is the customer journey. Are you tracking the *whole* safari you sent your buyer on? Are you ensuring your brand is top of mind early on? Are your transactions smooth and error-free? Do you follow up to ensure customer satisfaction and retention?

If the journey goes well, your customers will keep coming back. But make no mistake—all parts of the ride matter. CX is the whole shebang—from the first recognition of a need to the final follow-up message.

CX is also about the emotions generated along the way. Satisfaction, pleasure, appreciation—or, if you drop the ball, frustration, irritation, even rage.

So let's take a look at how we handle customer journeys.

ALL PAIN, NOT MUCH GAIN

How easy are we to do business with?

That question is a strategic one in today's world. But what does "customer ease" really mean? Think of it in two ways.

First, there's the *objective* time and effort customers spend during any encounter with your brand. Then there's the *subjective* perception—how easy they *feel* it is to deal with you. The lower the friction, both real and perceived, the greater the sense of ease your customers will feel.

The UK's Henley Business School has developed a handy framework. Remember the journey we talked about earlier? Customers engage with your brand at various stages: gathering info, buying, using products, and managing issues. If customers feel they're expending too much energy at any stage, your value diminishes. You've become too much effort to be worth their while.

Professor Moira Clark is Director of the Henley Centre for Customer Management. She identifies four types of energy customers expend when dealing with you, summed up in the acronym CEPT (pronounced "kept"):

- Cognitive energy: the mental effort customers use to figure out your offerings or make decisions
- Emotional energy: anxiety, stress, or frustration caused by interactions with your company

- Physical energy: the literal effort of coming to your premises or dealing with heavy items
- Time energy: that precious commodity—how long it takes to wait, transact, or use your offering

Feeling a little uneasy? You should be. Does your company confuse its customers with jargon? Frustrate them with poor service? Make them travel unnecessarily or wait forever? Then you're scoring low on ease—and that's going to cost you.

Use CEPT to map out your customer journeys and find those unnecessary pain points. And this applies just as much to those who sell to businesses. Every department you have must make it easy for customers to deal with you, period.

Customer journey mapping and CEPT are powerful tools for understanding and improving CX. They show you not only where you might be causing unnecessary pain but also where you can surprise and delight your customers. The journey is a way to track both your CX actions and the emotions they generate. Once you understand the feelings involved, fixing the issues becomes much easier.

THE *X* IN *CX*

Now we can get to the heart of the matter.

The X factor in CX, as you've already read, is the

culture and habits that allow you to attain sustained excellence in your customer interactions.

Where does that culture come from, and how do we turn it into a set of high-impact daily habits?

I have asked myself that question for decades. Why do just a few organizations attain customer excellence, while the majority just wallow in me-too mediocrity?

Here is my answer, based on years of observation and study, and through working in the boardrooms and trenches of business.

Those who master CX practice four things:

- First, they *boss it*—they start with the leaders, because the fire and passion for CX must come from the top.
- Second, they *humanize it*—they work resolutely on employee happiness, because only a happy team can produce happy customers.
- Third, they *digitize it*—they deploy the best digital tools smartly, to speed things up, reduce frictions, and personalize their offerings.
- Fourth, they *jazz it*—they know that the best CX is jazz, not a symphony, and they make their CX music original and creative.

Let's be clear: These four practices aren't magic wands for instant CX success. But embrace them and you're far more likely to deliver the best possible experience for your customers.

The next four chapters of this book will take each of the four practices—boss it, humanize it, digitize it, and jazz it—in turn.

Shall we?

4

Boss It

To lead people, walk beside them. As for the best leaders, the people do not notice their existence. When the best leader's work is done, the people say, "We did it ourselves!"

—Lao Tzu

In any collective endeavor, where does success begin? You know the answer: It begins at the top.

- Where are mere aspirations turned into determined missions?
- Where are standards set? Where are they enforced?
- Where are decisions made about focus and resourcing?
- Where is the motivation of the collective managed?

At the top.

Bosses make great CX a central part of strategy and mission. Bosses set customer standards at the top of organizations. Bosses recruit, train, and deploy employees to face customers. Bosses decide how much to spend to make things better. Bosses design processes. Bosses create response and recovery mechanisms. Bosses motivate employees to care about what happens to customers.

If the bosses do all that badly, then you get car-crash CX.

When we get angry as customers, whom should we be angry with? It's tempting to take it out on the frontline person we are dealing with directly, but the real culprits sit elsewhere. Very bad—and very good—customer experience is usually about the bosses, at all levels.

If you're experiencing bad service as a customer, don't take it out on the person in front of you. They are very likely underpaid, undertrained, and just doing their best in a bad situation. Even if the service representative you are dealing with is unpleasant or incompetent, the true fault lies elsewhere—in those who install inappropriate frontline staff and then fail to train and monitor them.

It is very easy for higher-ups to blame bad employees and bad tech for their CX woes. A better place to find the culprit would be in the mirror.

A weak business just states "customer centricity" as one of its core values (yawn—who doesn't these days) and then looks away and hopes for the best.

Let's be fair, consistently great CX is one of the

hardest things to pull off. It requires superhuman effort and attention to detail, as well as remarkable process efficiency. It is about talent, culture, technology, and innovation—all going hand in hand. Glitches and fails will occur—and must be forgiven. What is harder to forgive is disdain and lip service from the top, as well as CX blurbs that are all talk and no walk.

Great CX, then, begins with a leader who actually cares deeply about it. It is then embedded in the overarching strategy of the business, or it is just empty talk.

Jeff Bezos, Amazon's founder, put customers at the heart of his trailblazing company from the very beginning. The very first of Amazon's famed Leadership Principles demands that its leaders be obsessed with customers: Start with the customer and work backward.

When Bezos was pushing his team to develop the Kindle e-book reader, he made them work backward exactly like that: by imagining the customer experience first. It was strategically important for Amazon to move into the devices game, but they had to get their first e-reader right. It had to be easy on the eye, light in the hand, low on battery consumption, and able to download electronic books quickly and cheaply. The first Kindle shipped with those attributes and became a runaway success from day one.

Everything about excellent customer experience starts at the top. Whenever you observe outstanding CX, peer behind the curtain and you will also see outstanding leadership at work. For happy customers to be the norm and not the exception, both the people who head service delivery and those who head the entire organization have to care a great deal.

In other words, customer excellence has to be a cause and a passion for the folks at the top, not just a job. It has to be felt, not just designed and delivered. For the best bosses, customers' smiles and appreciations create a warm glow; complaints are registered as stinging rebukes.

If the bosses don't care enough, no one will. If the bosses lead the cheers and set the example, there's a chance others will follow.

How high should we go to look for the CX leader?

An excellent business sets CX standards at the level of the shareholder and board of directors, no less, and then recruits and invests accordingly.

This runs counter to the regular practices of big businesses. Customer care is something to be delegated, surely. It is done by the infantry, not the generals. Chief executives and boards can't preoccupy themselves with the minutiae of customer experience, can they?

They can, and should.

Let's return to the sentiments I began this book with.

Customers are the lifeblood of the business. They are the only part of the scheme putting money on the table every day. The rest—shareholders, employees, suppliers, governments—just extract. Customers pay for everything. Without them, we are toast. There are no corner offices, no fancy cars, no pay raises, no paying for school fees, no savings.

That is—or should be—a statement of the obvious.

Why, then, do we not see customers as the single most important stakeholder, the most vital cog in the machine? Why do the leaders of business imagine there are many more important things for them to be doing, other than making sure customers are being looked after and are locked in place for the long term?

Customers are the lifeblood of the business. They are the only part of the scheme putting money on the table every day.

I hope you are in no doubt: The chief executive officer of the business is also customer agent 001.

But wait, you say. CEOs have so much to do. Meeting business targets, quarter by quarter. Managing their shareholders and boards. Meeting government bigwigs. Crafting five-year plans. Worrying about risks. Keeping team spirit high throughout the organization. Playing golf . . .

Surely customer care is best left to underlings, whose actual job it is to ensure customers are happy and keep buying?

Absolutely not.

The CEO's job, in a nutshell, is to keep customers happy, by keeping employees happy. All other stakeholders are subservient; they get their payoffs if and only if you have happy employees serving happy customers.

What does this mean at a practical level, though? Is it just a nice catchphrase, to be customer agent number one? Or is there some way of making it true, every day?

CX AND THE CEO

Sam Walton was famous for trooping up and down supermarket aisles, watching his customers, interacting with them, logging which store parking lots were full and which were empty—and why. He did this almost to his dying day, so seriously did he take it.

Steve Jobs understood that Apple's mojo lay in the ease of use of its products. He urged his people to make computers that his grandmother could use—because he knew that CX at Apple was predicated on making stuff that anyone could get going with, no manual needed.

Richard Branson doesn't leave CX to others; he is well known for meeting random customers personally and chatting away, picking up insights to plug back into the business higher up.

Satya Nadella's cultural transformation of Microsoft has changed the performance review system to reward good behavior with customers, at all levels.

Oracle's Safra Catz has purposefully transformed the company, moving it from a product-focused approach to one that puts the customer first, with an emphasis on building personal relationships.

East African Breweries' Jane Karuku relentlessly pushes her senior people—and herself—to be in the bars where people drink—watching, chatting, and making notes.

Securex East Africa's founder Tony Sahni was for years personally available for every customer with a security problem. This helped him build the deep relationships that powered his fledgling firm into the region's leading security provider.

I hope these examples give you clear insight: "Bossing the CX" is about both the small things and the big things.

The small stuff is about setting the example for the organization. When you are on the ground meeting customers and shooting the breeze with them, you send out a very strong signal: *This stuff really matters around here—just look at the boss, always doing it.* The standard comes from you, and it must be reemphasized daily.

The big stuff is about connecting the dots for everyone and embedding customer primacy right into the heart of your strategy. It is about constructing a customer-excellence machine that does great CX as a matter of course.

You have to do both. You must be highly visible to both customers and employees, and you must also detach from the details to be more strategic and create systems, processes, and teams that look after customers naturally and continuously.

Here's a practical guide to the CX duties of the CEO:

Be your company's best customer. Steve Jobs is probably the most-studied CEO of all time. But one thing about him was always hidden in plain sight: He loved his products as a consumer, not just as a producer. He loved handling them, feeling them, working with them. He was *cliente número uno.* Steve Jobs's great achievement was to think like a customer. He intuitively understood what consumers would want, and what type of simplicity would blow them away. How many times is that true for others? Most CEOs are professional managers who may never consume their own product. The only passion they feel for it is in analyzing its sales and contribution to the bottom line. Often, CEOs are so detached from their products that their target customer is a mysterious figure to them, viewed even with derision. So wherever possible, you must eat your own dog food—and improve it through usage.

Be intentional about time. If spending more time with customers is way down on your list of priorities, let's be honest—it won't happen. You have to mark out time on your calendar for this. I would suggest at least an afternoon every week, or two full days every month, as the minimum time you should dedicate to meeting customers. Whom should you meet? Randomize this process as much as possible; otherwise, you will get skewed data. Just spend the time. Don't turn these sessions with customers into selling visits or marketing meetings—just show up and talk and listen, and see what happens.

Don't avoid the troublemakers. We all have awkward customers, and it's very human to avoid talking to them. That's where Bill Gates's observation kicks in: "Your most unhappy customers are your greatest source of learning." Don't shy away from the perennial complainers. Treat them as a huge learning experience and show your people how you deal with them personally and fix things. And if a small percentage of your customers are truly awful and a drain on everyone's time and enthusiasm, lead the way in dumping them. Show your staff where the line is drawn, and let the worst customers go to torment your competitors . . .

Know that happy customers come from happy employees. To have a strong customer relationship, most of your time must go to building a strong employee relationship. There is no way you can deal with more than very few customers, personally. You would be burnt out in a week—and you would neglect your many other duties. You have to create the team that does the CX, routinely and to a high standard. How does that happen? By engaging them deeply in the business and being the "coach of coaches"—passing the good practices down through continuous on-the-job training. It is perhaps paradoxical: To work on better relations with your customers, spend most of your time with your employees.

Bank on technology. Most of customer excellence is about human relationships. Customers need to have feelings about your products and people, and those feelings are usually the glue that makes them stick around for a long time. But never forget: Technology has a key role to play. Technology is turbocharging speed and convenience by removing frictions from customer journeys. Relationships are elevated by wow moments, and a customer who is pleasantly surprised by the speed of your delivery, or by useful features in your product, isn't going anywhere. It is your job to keep asking what technology could do to make everyone's work faster and easier—and to keep investing in it.

Be surprising. If you're going to be the role model, you must make your people wake up and take notice. A good way to do this is to be where you were not expected to be. In my time as a CEO advisor, I have pushed leaders to answer the telephones, sit at branch counters, work the reception desk, serve the food. Because no one expects you to do it, it gets noticed—and never forgotten. Make a point of doing this every so often, showing up to do the customer-facing work that your employees normally do. By doing it, you send an amazing message to two constituencies: employees and customers. That message? *We take customers very, very seriously around here—led by customer agent number one!*

Don't make CX your day job. Do make sure you don't take up all the oxygen in the room. You hopefully have competent professionals handling your customers, and you must leave the essential work to them—most of the time. Your fundamental role is to draw attention to the importance of their work, and to help them do it better. It's a smart dance, being agent number one: you show up in front of customers frequently, just to make the point and gather knowledge, but not so frequently that you make it all about you.

Bossing CX is about two key things: setting the standard and building the machine. Setting a high standard requires intentional visibility from you—you must be seen to really care about the customer experience. Building the machine is a more reflective pursuit. It requires you to step back a little and work on both staff engagement and technological acceleration. The long-term magic in CX comes from those two priorities—and they are the focus of the next two chapters in this book.

BOSS THE FRONT LINE

One of my most interesting assignments as a young strategy consultant was working with a US disaster management agency in Hawaii to formulate its strategy. This agency was owned by the US Pacific Command, so my first task was to spend a day interviewing, among others, a general and a colonel at their Hawaii base. Those conversations were some of the most enlightening of my career. I left realizing how crucial leadership is—perhaps even more so than strategy itself.

A thought-provoking idea from that experience: "In great armies, the job of generals is to back up their sergeants." Colonel Tom Wilhelm, quoted in Tom Peters's *Excellence Now: Extreme Humanism*, highlights a crucial point about leadership that corporate organizations often miss—success hinges on the frontline leaders, not just those at the top.

Right now, I'm addressing the generals reading this book—make no mistake, great customer experience depends on how well you lead your sergeants.

Frontline leaders, those managing the first line of employees, are the sergeants of your organization.

Too often, we pour our attention into senior leaders, assuming that leadership at lower levels matters less. That's wrong. The real challenge is for top leaders to inspire and organize those who run things at the place where the actual work is done.

In an airline, the CEO's work is meaningless if the supervisors leading the cleaning and maintenance teams are weak. A dirty tray table immediately makes a customer wonder what other standards are slipping. Banks are the same—strategy discussions at the top are pointless if branch managers can't lead effectively.

Bossing CX is about two key things: setting the standard and building the machine.

The truth is, leadership matters at every level. So why do we focus all our energy and training budgets on the top leaders? Frontline supervisors hold the keys to productivity, quality, and employee retention—yet they're often neglected.

It's time to embrace the front line. If your sergeants are great leaders, you'll see the results everywhere—better CX, stronger culture, and improved safety. If not, your strategy will fall flat, and a toxic culture may take root.

So how do you elevate frontline leadership? First, get down there. Spend time with your frontline teams, listen, and act quickly on what you find. Recruitment matters too—don't fill frontline positions with anyone available; find people with leadership potential. Invest in their development by delivering in-house, on-the-job training, and letting good managers mentor new ones. And most importantly, respect them. Frontline leaders should feel valued by the organization's top brass.

Remember: The CX buck stops with the CEO. You're responsible for how customers are treated and for how your frontline leaders are supported.

As Tom Peters says, losing top officers would be tough, but losing sergeants would be catastrophic.

CX AND THE BOARD

The board of directors? Surely that's pushing it? The board, that esteemed group, can't be involved in customer care—those duties belong to managers.

But wait.

Blockbuster. Kodak. Nokia. BlackBerry. What do they have in common? They all failed to grasp shifts in customer preferences.

Apple. Samsung. Netflix. Amazon. Zara. Shein. Spotify. What's their common feature? A laser-like focus on customers. They understand needs before customers do, and obsess over every CX detail, creating wow moments through quality, value, or convenience.

Standout business successes come from close customer scrutiny. Safaricom saw M-PESA's potential by watching—and leading—its customers. Equity Bank thrived by focusing on overlooked customers. East African Breweries made it to one hundred years of existence by refreshing its portfolio in line with consumption trends. Securex grew because its founders obsessed with early customers and were always available for them.

Customers, in short, can make or break you.

So why wouldn't the board of directors be all over this fact?

Your biggest threat is your customer. If you miss their shifting habits, you're creating a slow puncture that will leave you (and your company) in a ditch.

Your biggest opportunity? Your customer. If you stay ahead of them, like Amazon or Netflix, you'll be ready for their next destination. If they love interacting with your products, as with Apple or Samsung, they'll stick with you for life.

There's nothing more strategic for business than customers. Even my local corner shop knows this—it is growing rapidly by meeting rising demand for delivery and special services.

Do big businesses grasp this point? The upper echelons are usually too removed from customers, relying on filtered reports. Yet excelling with customers must begin at the top.

So who's fighting for the customer at the highest level—the boardroom?

Boards are good at many things—keeping the financials, risks, and compliance in check. They approve marketing, monitor sales, and even focus on talent management.

The customer sits beneath every aspect of the business—strategy, revenue, risk, and compliance. So who is truly speaking for the customer at the board table? All the board members? Or none?

Customers must be dragged to the center of the board's agenda.

It's true that delivering great CX is everyone's job—from the top to the guards, cleaners, and delivery teams. The whole business is a customer-satisfaction machine. But focus is needed at all levels, starting with the board. Every company that excels at CX does so from the top. That's where the standards are set and where going the extra mile for customers is made a priority.

Customer issues must be discussed at the board level. Boards must understand customer journeys. But do please proceed with caution.

How might we do this? Give the head of CX a board seat? Set up a new committee? Cram customer discussions into every meeting? These solutions may have pitfalls.

Some suggest leaving an empty chair for the customer in the boardroom, but that's a bit gimmicky. We can do better.

First, your board needs to understand why customers are vital. Keeping a close eye on customers touches every part of the business: strategy, risk, compliance,

IT, sales, and talent. The board can't ignore customers or leave them to others.

If the *why* is clear, let's move to the *how*. Start by selecting directors with experience in studying and serving customers. If no one has that expertise, the conversation won't happen.

Next, mine your customer data for insights. Make customer analytics a key part of board discussions.

Boards should also interact with customers directly. I encourage directors to spend time with customers before board meetings. It enriches the discussions. Organize customer panels, meet and greets, or events that bring customers and directors together. This gives boards a more intimate understanding of customer issues.

Make customer topics mandatory at least twice a year in board meetings. Without this, directors will only touch customer issues superficially.

Directors must also experience the customer journey themselves. A bank's directors should use the bank's services. A manufacturer's directors should buy and use their products. Only then can they walk in the customer's shoes and gain real insight. Chairs should insist on it.

For fast-changing consumer behavior, bring in external experts. Sometimes the future is hard to see from within, and futurists can help boards understand emerging customer trends.

But remember: Boards should engage with customer matters strategically, not micromanage. Directors should sniff around customer issues, but not take charge of them. Their knowledge should elevate the discussion, not be used to bash managers.

To sum up: Bring the loud voice of the customer into the boardroom. Customers are the reason your business exists. They put money on the table every day, and that money pays for everything. Stay close to your customers, stay ahead of them, and hold them for life. We all know this, but customer discussions are still rare in boardrooms.

Every company that excels at CX does so from the top. That's where the standards are set and where going the extra mile for customers is made a priority.

Let's make customers central to boardroom discussions.

Kenneth B. Elliott asked us to regard customers not as interruptions to our work but as the purpose of it. Apply this to your board. Customers are the purpose of your work.

BOSS THE CULTURE

Let's review everything that's been recommended in this chapter thus far. What if the following things are happening in your business?

- The CEO leads CX from the front—and is a visible and active participant in CX delivery.
- Frontline leaders—those who lead the customer-facing teams—are respected and made prominent in the organization.
- The board of directors, no less, takes CX very seriously, embeds it into the strategy of the business, and reviews CX performance regularly.

Guess what you will also have achieved: You'll boss the culture.

Culture is every organization's social glue. It is what binds people together in a shared endeavor. When people behave and react in similar ways to shared challenges, that's a culture at work. And culture is unbelievably powerful.

I was once in Germany, on its famed Autobahn, chatting with my local driver. I saw him tense up. He asked me in an exasperated voice, "Did you just see that?" I had indeed seen it. A BMW driver had joined the highway ahead of us, blending in smoothly with the vehicles already present. He had used his indicator early to signal his intentions, before joining the stream of cars. All was well, I thought.

Not for my driver, who was furious. "He's supposed to use his indicator and *then wait* for me to flash my headlights to confirm that it's okay for him to come in ahead of me. He never did that! I'm noting his registration and I'll be reporting him after we stop!"

Yikes, I thought. Now that's strict. But where does it come from, and why does the driver feel so invested in road safety? From the culture, of course. Germans want everything to be orderly and efficient. They detest disorder and lack of discipline. They have not only the world's most well-organized roads; they also make the most well-engineered cars in the world. For decades. Why? Because there's a self-enforcing culture at work.

Why is Singapore so clean and orderly, when many of its neighbors live in noisy daily tumult?

Why is Kigali the only really clean city in East Africa?

Why do the Italians make some of the planet's best food and fashion?

Why do some companies pull off sustained excellence in CX, while their competitors struggle to keep up?

The answer, in all cases, is the culture.

My last book, *Up & Ahead,* was about strategy. In it I wrote this: "Strategy is what you think you'll do; culture is what you'll actually do."

This applies to your CX strategy too. Does your strategy require folks to be warm and friendly, quick and responsive? Well, you'd better have the culture for it. People behave in preset ways, ways defined by their culture. If you can't reset the culture, the presets will keep running. Culture exerts a really powerful pull on the group, because we are social creatures who respond to social conditioning. We observe others, we mimic them, and we cooperate with them. We gain status from being prominent members of our group, and to be prominent is to be the culture carrier.

The culture and habits that drive the best CX come firstly from the bosses.

Where does it come from, this all-powerful culture? Most forcefully, from the leaders. From *Up & Ahead*, again: "Leaders influence culture more than anyone else. The example they set matters more than anything else. Their behaviors set the tone for everyone else. The workforce's sense of what is important and what is rewarded comes from observation of leaders."

If everyone from the board to the C-suite to middle managers to frontline leaders can set a powerful example around required behaviors, and employees can be rewarded and appreciated for living those behaviors, then great CX can happen for you.

The culture and habits that drive the best CX come firstly from the bosses. Once you've bossed the culture—by exemplifying it—you're ready to move on to the next CX practice: paying deep attention to the humans.

5 Humanize It

Customers will never love a company until the employees love it first.

—Simon Sinek

If you're not looking after the people who look after your customers, you can forget about your CX.

That is so obviously true, yet it is flabbergasting how many bosses miss it.

You can't order or direct great CX. You have to inspire it.

If your normal practice is to treat your people as mere expendable resources, paying them as little as you can get away with, and supervising them like recalcitrant children, then seriously, you can put this book down now.

Or you can continue, and pay heed to this piece of

advice from John DiJulius: "Your customers will never be happier than your employees."

In other words, the goal of happy customers must come from the strategy of happy employees.

This is just plain common sense. Unhappy people can't make anyone happy. Misery loves company, and misery is spread easily. When you're a customer having a difficult conversation with an employee, you can tell from that person's demeanor and body language how engaged they are with their work. As customers, we have to deal with underpaid and undertrained employees all the time. It's no fun. Sometimes those miserable employees are right in front of us—at reception desks or checkout counters—and sometimes they're being unhappy behind the curtain, manning the systems and processes meant to make our lives easier. Predictably, the CX we encounter will be *meh* at best. Unhappy employees put in their minimum effort, and no more.

JUST TWO THINGS

What if I told you that your business should focus most of its attention on just *two* things? Success in a competitive business can indeed be boiled down to two fundamentals.

Businesses must, of course, deliver increasing shareholder value. Without that, there will be no future—the rug will be pulled, the lights will be switched off. As CEO, you are measured by your numbers: top line, bottom line, growth, margins, dividends. But businesses should also add real value to the world in two more fundamental ways: by giving purpose and achievement and meaning to their employees, and by giving satisfaction and utility and joy to their customers.

A business that is merely a vehicle for the personal enrichment of a tiny subgroup of society is not going to have any meaningful impact in the world. Its owners will lead a small life, and its employees and customers will not gain any meaning from their interactions with the organization.

If you are interested in knowing how close to true achievement your business is, consider my two essential tests of business success.

The first test relates to customers, and it is this: *Do your customers recommend your company's products to their relatives and very best friends?* In other words, does your organization bring good news to its customers, news so good that they want to spread it to those who are closest to them?

It is in the nature of human beings to want to share good tidings and good things with those who matter to them. And that is the real test for your products and user experiences: whether they matter enough in the lives of those who consume them that they want their nearest and dearest to partake in the goodness.

The second test relates to the nature of the employee experience: *Is this the organization everyone in your industry wants to work for?* Note that this test does not ask whether this is the company that pays the best or gives out the most perks (I have seen plenty of those in my time, and their employees are often no better engaged than the norm).

The second test is not about money; it is about how good it is to work for you. Do employees relish the experience, do they feel involved and appreciated, do they feel like they're growing in their personal impact? Do they give their best efforts to their work? And do those who don't work for you wish they did?

So these are the two big concerns for the board and CEO: Are my employees happy, and are my customers happy?

Wait, did we leave the shareholders out? If they are unhappy, they'll make everyone unhappy! Well, here's the thing: When you can engage properly with your staff and get the best work of which they are capable out of them, and when you can bond so well with customers that they are with you for life and will rope in lots of others, the bottom line will take care of itself.

Do your employees love working for you, truly? Do your customers love buying from you, truly? These are tough tests, make no mistake. Very few organizations have any hope of meeting them. But that doesn't mean your business should not pass muster. Make it your mission to be the one that does.

Andrew Chamberlain and Daniel Zhao ran a study comparing employee satisfaction and customer satisfaction for the *Harvard Business Review* in 2019. They asked this question: Can companies help to achieve high customer satisfaction by investing in employees and ensuring that those who deliver goods and services are themselves satisfied with their jobs?

They found a strong statistical link between employee well-being (reported on Glassdoor) and customer satisfaction among a big sample of some of the largest companies. They concluded that a happier workforce is clearly associated with companies' ability to deliver better customer satisfaction—particularly in industries with the closest contact between workers and customers, including retail, tourism, restaurants, health care, and financial services.

As a business leader, you should think about two groups every day: your people, and the people they serve. If you have highly engaged people delivering great customer experiences and value, then you have every chance of being a great success, for a long time.

Also, be very afraid. The quickest way to come undone as a business is to have your employees or customers turn on you. Never take those two groups for granted. Don't think they are dispensable and replaceable. It takes a lot of work to rebuild teams and to find new customers. Have some healthy paranoia with you all the time: *This whole thing could tank if I don't keep watching the employee experience and the customer experience.* That paranoia will keep you ahead of the game.

WHERE HAPPY HUMANS WORK

Where do we find happy customers created by happy employees? It's worth looking at some of the companies that have this figured out.

Zappos wrote the book on customer care at an online business. Selling shoes on the internet? No one thought that possible until Zappos showed everyone how to do it. Great CX was embedded into the firm's strategy from day one. What's the secret? It's the culture. Zappos gives employees authority to not only resolve customer problems but to introduce innovations that make CX better. Zappos offers ease of ordering, no-hassle returns, and quick interactions. That's all come from a culture of service, not from a rule book. This culture makes employees want to play their part in the company's success—and that's what's unusual. Zappos *only* wants employees who can feel like they belong—their culture is that important to them.

Let's move on to Disney, a more mature business famed for its theme parks that have become magical tourist destinations for families. There's a different magic going on behind the scenes: that of making employees believe they work in a truly special place—and want to keep working there. In other words, the staff feel the magic too, not just the customers. This sense of belonging is key to employee engagement. People feel most comfortable, and most able to dig deep when it comes to hard work, when they feel *This is my place; these are my people.* When they don't feel that, they're just marking time.

Luxury retailer Nordstrom is also renowned for service—and that comes squarely from its employees. One of their key methods of finding those employees comes from recruitment. Or, as Nordstrom famously puts it: "Hire the smile, train the skill." As former president and chairman Bruce Nordstrom explains it, he can hire nice people and train them to sell, but he can't hire salespeople and train them to be nice! In other words, they look for nice people first, because it really matters. There are not a lot of formal training programs going on at Nordstrom. When Bruce Nordstrom was asked about who then trains the staff, his answer was both profound and hilarious: "Their parents."

Nordstrom's approach is to give people a reason to come to work excited—because there you will find opportunity, freedom, being valued as a person, and connecting to something meaningful.

When Bruce Nordstrom was asked about who then trains the staff, his answer was both profound and hilarious: "Their parents."

Hire the smile, train the skill. That is such a profound observation about where great CX comes from. I have been telling my CEO clients for decades now: *When you meet smilers, hire them!* People with a sunny disposition are really rare. We all like them when we meet them, because they cheer us up. And yet when we are hiring, we become preoccupied with qualifications and experience, even when we are looking for people to put in front of customers. I wish I were in the room when you're interviewing a happy person and about to pass on them. I'd be shouting, *That's a smiler! Reconsider!* You can train them up on the rest of the stuff later. But natural smiles, every day? You can't train that.

(Of course, a smile alone doesn't cut it. We need our top customer-facing folks to not only have naturally lit-up faces but also be ethical and conscientious by nature. A smile that masks a lack of integrity or a slapdash approach to work is not what I am recommending.)

I recall an interesting interaction at an airport where I was checking in to fly with a well-known airline. The employee handling me wore a smiley button on her lapel. It said: "I smile." But she never did, not once, while checking me in. As she handed me my boarding pass, I asked her about the button. She scowled and told me all customer-facing staff were required to attend a customer-care training program, and the smiley buttons were handed out at the end, to become a part of their uniform. The airline had spent millions on the training.

"But it didn't work?" I asked. She scowled again, and asked me why she should smile if her employer paid her a pittance, imposed grueling schedules, and offered her little flexibility as a young mother. I sympathized and left.

You can't train smiles. You have to give your people a reason to smile.

THE STATE OF EMPLOYEE ENGAGEMENT

Employee engagement really matters, but we mostly do it badly. Gallup runs an annual State of the Global Workplace survey, and it usually makes for grim reading.

Over recent years, a pattern is discernible. Only one in five workers is actually engaged with their work—they feel involved, are enthusiastic, and go the extra mile. Three in five are typically not engaged, while one in five is actively disengaged.

Think about it: An average team of five workers has only *one* willing to do the work with any eagerness or gusto. Three are just showing up for the money and will give you none of their discretionary effort. One actually detests the organization and has already quit mentally.

It gets worse. More than half of employees are typically looking for a new job, or actively seeking to leave. That statistic is even worse in sub-Saharan Africa, where I do most of my work: Three-quarters of workers are open to or searching for new work.

I ask you: How well do you think these folks will serve your customers?

This lack of meaningful interest in work is very, very costly. Enthusiasm is one of the key ingredients of success, and always has been. There is only so much anyone can achieve when bored or bitter or benumbed. And as Gallup points out, negative emotions from work end up at home. If you're not thriving at work, you're unlikely to be thriving at life. So what are we getting wrong, people?

The typical manager's knee-jerk response to these figures is to decry the state and nature of the workers. See? Employees are work-shy, disloyal slackers. There's nothing you can do with most of them.

I beg to differ. As I wrote years ago in my book *The Bigger Deal*, stop blaming the employees! Most people are not lazy crooks or impossible to manage. They do come to life—somewhere. They do give of their best—somewhere. Where? Often, it's in the other projects of their lives: their families, their faiths, their communities—even their sports teams. If we want them to come to life at work, the onus is on us.

There are, of course, bad employees that none of us can do anything with. But that's a small proportion. What do the middle group—the 60 percent who could be engaged, but aren't—want? Gallup asked that question: What would make your workplace better? Only 28 percent globally thought it was about being paid more—and even those had nuances like being paid on time, being paid on merit, and sharing rewards more equally. The majority wanted improvements relating to culture and well-being: recognition for work; open dialogue; autonomy in decision-making; learning and growth; fairness; flexibility; social spaces; and plain, simple respect.

There's a clear message there: Make the workplace more human, and the humans will come to work.

There are organizations that know this very well.

Those who win Gallup's Exceptional Workplace Awards are very different. The global average is about one engaged employee for every one actively disengaged employee. But for the good workplaces, that ratio is eighteen to one. That's a huge difference.

Where to begin if we want to be better? At heart, this is a failure of management and leadership. Gallup estimates that 70 percent of team engagement is attributable to the manager. Bad managers make bad teams and bad employees. But do we even bother to teach managers how to lead human beings? We teach them to meet targets and run a tight ship, certainly—but the human part? How to create the conditions in which humans can thrive? How to understand the mass—and mess—of feelings that is the human being, and how to harness and channel the energy in those feelings? Not so much.

In *The Bigger Deal* I called it a shameful waste of life and talent, to be employed like that and to be employing like that. We still persist with workplace models that are from feudal times and from primitive factories. To get the best out of them, we must celebrate people as people.

Here's an experience someone close to me recounted. He had gone to a leading retailer to buy a laptop. He had chosen the model. He had the money. He was ready to take it home.

Oops. It turned out the shop didn't actually have the item, even though their website had confirmed it was in stock. The assistant promised to find the laptop from another branch and get back to the customer.

We know what happened next; don't we?

They never got back. My friend was flabbergasted. "Do these folks not want to make a sale?" he asked me. "Don't they want to make money?"

This is not fundamentally an employee problem; it's a leadership problem. It is a problem of bad jobs and bad bosses. Very few humans want to be in jobs they hate; they are there out of desperation, not by choice.

What makes so many jobs bad? Primitive work design. Poor pay. Little or no training. Use of fear rather than hope as a key motivator. Next to no team spirit or kinship with fellow employees. No prospects for advancement. In these bad jobs, the only reason people work is to earn their daily bread. They will leave at the first real opportunity.

Those folks ain't calling anyone back.

Make the workplace more human, and the humans will come to work.

If you want great customer experience, first deliver great employee experience. Reward competitively, or at least fairly. Train people, in both skills and behaviors.

Show them how. Set the example from the top. Show a path to personal advancement. Give them a stake in the success of the business. Have fun together.

If your staff members are happy, your customers have some possibility of also being happy. If your employees are generally unhappy, there is no such possibility.

Is a happy and engaged workplace too much for you to pull off, leaders? Then go ahead, leave all the money on the table. Work with people who detest you. Treat them like beasts of burden rather than humans with hopes and feelings. Never smile, let alone laugh, with your employees. Make insincere promises.

Count your money, for it won't be lasting long.

Boards and senior executives spend huge amounts of time and money on strategy, operations, technology, efficiency, and the like. But all of those are achieved through human beings. If we can't work well with humans, we can only achieve short-lived success. Proper managers don't just manage deadlines and deliverables; they manage feelings. They succeed because they build teams that want to succeed.

These skills can be trained and coached. They are teachable. But the imperative must come from the top. If the senior-most folks just see resources when they gaze down upon the organization, there is no hope that anyone else will see *people.*

This is about fundamental values. Do we believe that our real work as leaders is to grow humans, who will in turn grow the organization? Or is it just to grow the bottom line, any which way we can?

HOW TO GENERATE THE SMILES

I was sitting in a restaurant looking at a sushi menu some time back. There were many delectable-sounding options on offer, and I wondered what to choose. I decided to ask a server for advice. Here's what she said: "Please try the chef's signature sushi roll. He thought long and hard about it and experimented with various ingredients and created some final options. He asked all the restaurant staff to try it out and vote on a winner. We all chose this one, sir. Please try it—it's really wonderful."

Her enthusiasm was infectious, so I immediately tried the chef's special. It was indeed special.

I would like you to read her words again. In that quote is contained the essence of employee engagement.

The restaurant in question was in the Oberoi hotel in Mumbai, and it had a battalion of waiters swirling around, all looking thoroughly engaged with their work. It was endearing to learn that the waitstaff work in tandem with the kitchen staff, that their opinions are sought on the quality of the food, that they enjoy the same food they serve, and that their jobs are not dismissed as lowly. That's something every leader on the planet should learn: There are no high or low members of the organization. Rewards and responsibilities differ, of course they do; but no one should feel disengaged and disenchanted. For excellence to happen and be felt by customers, it must be delivered from top to bottom.

Employee engagement really matters. Gallup tells us why. There is strong evidence from their surveys that decreasing the number of disengaged workers drives positive outcomes within organizations. In 2024 it conducted a meta-analysis with data from 183,500 business units across 53 industries and 90 countries. The upshot? High-engagement business units get markedly better outcomes.

The negatives go down: Absenteeism, staff turnover, theft, safety incidents, and quality defects all show marked reductions when teams are well engaged.

The positives go up: customer loyalty, employee productivity, employee well-being, and organizational participation.

And the bottom line is better: All of that adds up to higher profits.

So how is it done, this wonderful thing that makes employees feel and work better, customers feel and spend better, and shareholders feel and gain better?

It is done by humanizing your workplace. It makes me a little sad to write that, because the implication is that we have had dehumanized workplaces for eons. The good news is that as humans we should be able to understand easily what it takes to bring the humanity back to our offices and factories.

Based on a lifetime of watching and working with organizations, let me offer some powerful ways to humanize what happens at work.

The first imperative is to recruit and develop better managers. Having a bad manager—an incompetent, a bully, or a constant critic—is one of the most dispiriting experiences in life. If we want to get better at employee engagement, we absolutely must get better at managing those employees. That means we must screen out all the bad hires through more perceptive and more innovative selection methods, and we must develop and promote differently.

Bad managers are often good at kissing up and kicking down—and that in itself is a red flag. If someone is over-jolly and extra-helpful with their bosses, watch out to see if that behavior continues when they leave the room and take the elevator down. CEOs and HR heads must be extra-vigilant if they want to root out bad-boss behavior on the ground. Giving our people good supervisors is one of the most powerful levers we can pull if we want to boost customer engagement. And as good humans, we owe it to the humans we employ not to place them in the care of head honchos who harass or oppress them.

We also have to train and deploy those managers better. Way too many managers in the world still think that managing others is all about command and control, as though they are running the plantations of times past. In a modern setting, managers need to behave more like coaches: understanding their people and drawing the best out of them. That's a very different game from rank and yank, or demand and command.

Leadership experts Herminia Ibarra and Anne Scoular pointed out in the *Harvard Business Review* in 2019 that managers need full institutional support to reinvent themselves as coaches, whose real job is "to draw energy, creativity, and learning out of the people with whom they work." Very well said, and a major challenge for the HR function. But individual managers can also read this and do something about it.

The team is before you, and you are the coach. What do you need to know?

Team performance has been extensively researched, and we know a great deal about what makes teams of all types—sports teams, military units, business start-ups—fly or fall. Here's my summary of the four essences of coaching/leading your teams:

1. **Safety:** Top coaches make sure every player knows they have their back. They are fair and consistent in their handling of the team, and don't play favorites. They give every player the psychological safety to grow and give of their best. They don't tolerate prolonged failure, but they are fair in their judgments and give people every chance to improve.
2. **Cause:** The best coaches don't just play it one game at a time (or one financial quarter at a time), nor do they treat achievement as just personal rewards and incentives. They demonstrate bigger deals to their players and enroll them in something more meaningful than the individual: the greatness of shared accomplishment, with wider impact. The best teams try to make history, not just money.

3. **Togetherness:** Teams work best when they have kinship and feel part of a community. Only the coach/leader can create the conditions in which team spirit flourishes. And as every coach knows, spirit can be a magical ingredient, one that overcomes deficiencies in skills and talent.
4. **Person:** The team may be a collective, but it consists of individuals—diverse, idiosyncratic, peculiar individuals. To get them to all play well together, great understanding of how brains are wired differently and how personalities differ is necessary. Great coaches are also great psychologists; they develop instinctive know-how of the differences in their people, and they sense how to deploy them so that they play to their strengths.

Study any team that has enjoyed sustained success, in any field of endeavor, and you will see these four essences in play.

Use the four essences to self-assess your coaching prowess. Do your people feel safe and fairly treated under your leadership? Do they feel connected to something bigger than themselves? Do they have fun together and forge unusual bonds? Do they appreciate your understanding of them as individuals?

Be a coach first and a boss second, and your impact as a leader can grow by an order of magnitude.

FIT FOR HUMANS

To sum up: What does a workplace fit for humans look like?

Asma Khan can tell you. A Bengali Muslim immigrant in the UK, she is a trained lawyer with a PhD in constitutional law. Yet her acclaim comes from a different realm entirely. Asma is famous for cooking the dishes of her childhood. She hadn't learned to cook when she got married and moved to England, only picking it up because she missed the flavors of home.

Starting small with supper clubs run from her home, she eventually opened her restaurant, Darjeeling Express, in central London. This all-woman kitchen is named after a train she rode during summer holidays as a child. Her cookbook *Asma's Indian Kitchen* became a bestseller, and she was featured on Netflix's *Chef's Table*, sealing her fame.

In a profile featured in the *Guardian* newspaper, Asma cemented her status not just as an elite chef but as a principled critic of the industry. She condemned a restaurant culture rife with bullying and abuse. She asked us all to condemn and boycott restaurants where there is bullying, racism, or sexual harassment, where staff don't feel safe.

Her impassioned denunciation is a call to action. It should make all businesses, not just restaurants, that mistreat their staff and exploit their labor hang their heads in shame.

Students of philosophy may have noticed that

Asma Khan echoes the sentiments of the renowned philosopher Immanuel Kant, who warned against using people as mere tools for achieving our own goals. Every human has inherent worth and should be given the respect and dignity we accord ourselves.

It's really as simple as that. A workplace that's fit for humans has dignity, fairness, and respect at its heart. Using those elements as essential design features would allow us to build organizations that customers feel warmth and affection for, and which can last for generations.

This is a book about customers, but the path to customers is created, cleared, and maintained by employees.

Ivan Menezes knew all about that.

Our paths crossed only briefly, when Diageo's global CEO was attending the centennial celebrations of East African Breweries—a Diageo subsidiary—in 2022. At dinner, we engaged in a captivating discussion on business, leadership, and strategy. I left with a renewed sense of optimism, realizing that a global CEO of a vast corporation could also be a good human.

This revelation stemmed from a poignant moment in our conversation. When I asked Ivan about his proudest accomplishment at Diageo, he said that it was this: successfully navigating the COVID-19 pandemic for two years without laying off a single employee. He personally championed a lifeline fund to protect the business, its brand, culture, and moral compass.

Few CEOs would prioritize protecting others alongside their professional triumphs. Make no mistake, Ivan was a decisive CEO with his eye very much on the bottom line. Early on in his tenure, he made some bold moves, right-sizing and refocusing the company. He flattened the management structure, empowered regional decision-making, shifted the business toward premium spirits, and reconnected leadership with consumers.

His efforts bore fruit, as Diageo's share price doubled during his tenure, solidifying its position among the FTSE 100 giants.

Ivan is sadly no more, but his deeds as an enlightened CEO live on. Why is being a kind, compassionate, and considerate person not more commonplace in the upper echelons of business? There seems to be a deep misconception that nice guys finish last, that displaying kindness gets you marked as soft, that bullying and braggadocio are essential ingredients of corporate success.

Well, please miss me with all that. If you think you

can only be successful by being avaricious, then I'd find you to be the least interesting of humans.

I have dedicated the past twenty years to focusing on one leader at a time to take them back to their essence: being true to their fundamental humanity. It is a slow and painful process, often with many unexpected reversals. But it is essential work.

This is a book about customers, but the path to customers is created, cleared, and maintained by employees. If you want to keep reaching your customers and keep earning their attention and patronage, look after those employees and inspire some zest and brio in them.

6 Digitize It

You've got to start with the customer experience and work back toward the technology—not the other way around.

—Steve Jobs

I've lived through not one but four monumental waves of computing technology, stretching from the 1980s to the present. Let's take a quick trip down memory lane.

When I started at university, computers lived in special rooms. You had to book a time slot just to use one, and even then, you never actually saw the thing itself—just a terminal with a flickering green screen in front of you. You had to know how to speak the machine's language, and for most of us, that meant we could do only the most basic of tasks.

By the time I graduated, the personal computer was breaking out into homes, schools, and small businesses. Sitting in front of one felt like being handed the keys to a mysterious new kingdom. Word processors, spreadsheets, and early presentation software were magical—but expensive, clunky, and slow. Software was basic, memory was laughable, and graphics were pixelated jokes.

Then came the laptop, and computing went mobile. My first job had a limited number of laptops to be shared; by the time I moved to my next role, every knowledge worker had their own. We became road warriors, armed with backpacks, able to work on the move.

But here's the catch: You could only work on what was on your machine, sharing stuff via floppy disks. Enter the second wave, an absolute tsunami—the internet.

Suddenly, an ocean of information opened up, and millions (eventually billions) were connected. The world shrank and everything seemed within reach. Email replaced postal mail, websites popped up everywhere, and e-commerce took off. We could now research anything and talk to anyone, anywhere—borderless life was unfolding.

Well, almost. Computers were still expensive, and internet speeds were painfully slow unless you paid through the nose for bandwidth.

Cue wave 3. The mobile phone, once just for calls, transformed human life even further. Apple's 2007 iPhone launch, Google's Android, and the arrival of app stores changed everything. Suddenly, we had the world in our hands—cameras, bank accounts, music collections, payment systems, and more—all in one device. Add cloud computing and better connectivity, and boom: supercomputers in our palms. Apps became the new currency, and social media took over our social lives. No more desks, no more borders. We could work, play, and connect from anywhere.

Now we're in wave 4: Artificial intelligence is embedding itself in everyday life. But that's a story for later in this chapter.

TAP, TAP, DONE

A few years ago I decided to change my cell phone number (don't ask).

Those who needed to know my new number needed to know it. So I made a list of those folks: family and friends, of course, but also colleagues, clients, banks, and other essential service providers.

Once the new SIM card was installed and seemed to be working well, I sat down with the office team to contact everyone on the list. We made calls and sent emails. High on the list were our two banks. I wrote to my relationship managers, informed them of the change, asked them to effect it on the bank systems immediately. They wrote back quickly, confirmed that the number would be updated and the old one deleted, and assured me of continued excellent service.

All good?

I think you know what happened next. How long do you think the banks took to update my phone number? In the case of the better bank (in this instance), six months of multiple phone calls. The second bank was still trying to call me on the old number eighteen months later! A very sheepish and frustrated relationship manager finally asked me if I could just send them an old-fashioned letter, signed in ink, asking them to change the number on the system. That was the only way to make sure it happened.

Fast-rewind. Exactly sixty minutes after the new SIM was first installed on my iPhone, it bleeped up a message saying something like: You have changed your SIM card. Do you wish this to become your permanent new number?

I tapped YES.

Another message: Do you want to make this your number across all your devices?

I tapped YES again.

Final message: Do you wish to keep or delete the old number?

I tapped DELETE.

All done, in seconds. And I never had to think about it again.

Contrast the two customer experiences. One involved months of back-and-forth communication, and important calls not being made because of my phone numbers being mixed up by the banks. It was frustrating, annoying, and time-consuming. The other was quick, automated, and effective. No human had to get involved, except me.

Tap, tap, done.

I have used that example to bash my banking

industry clients for years. In their defense, however, I must explain that they operate in one of the most tightly regulated industries. Compliance rules require them to keep strict control over customer data, and changing anything, even a phone number, requires multiple approvals. Their systems are designed to be difficult to update—better safe than sorry, they say.

I get it. And yet I now have a comparator for customer-experience excellence, and it's in the palm of my hand. Billions of us are now used to a digital world where many things can be done with two or three taps and swipes. We know what's possible, and we expect it of *everyone*.

So if you are still telling your customers to show up in person at your physical premises, if you are still asking them to fill in long-winded forms, if you are still taking days and weeks to respond to the simplest requests, then you're cruisin' for a bruisin'.

I note these days that Gen Z tries to give traditional banks a wide berth; that cohort of humans prefers to join digital-first, challenger banks that can sign them up right on the phone and get them transacting immediately. No showing your face in a branch to sign stuff, followed by a monthlong wait to have your account approved by some mysterious entity.

When digital experiences work really well, they overwhelm all things analogue, in speed and efficiency.

Consider this. Your smartphone has a powerful, handy camera on it, one that's with you all the time. That's changed photography completely. More photos are taken every two years these days than in the whole of human history since photography was invented. Why? It's the customer experience, of course. Before smartphone photography, how did you (or your parents) take photos?

First, you had to buy a camera. The better it was, the heavier and more expensive. Then you had to go to a store in person and buy photographic film, also expensive. Next, when you were ready to take some snaps, you had to insert that film into the camera. Easier said than done, some of you will recall—and if you got this part wrong, you might end up with no photos at all. Then you had to lug your camera around wherever you needed to take your photos. When you actually took one, you could only look through a viewfinder to frame the shot—you didn't see the actual photo until much later. Oh, and did I mention the film only gave you a small number of photos? Twelve, twenty-four, or thirty-six. So you had to choose what you wanted to photograph very carefully.

Snaps all taken? Not done yet. Now you had to carefully extract the film from the camera. Take it back to the photo store guy. Hand it in for processing—also expensive. And then wait several days for the photos to be developed and printed for you. When the photos were finally in your hand, the only way to show anyone your collection was to have them visit your home and look at your albums.

How much of a pain was that?

And these days? See something interesting, or even not interesting at all? Just pull your phone out and snap it. Take several shots and delete the bad ones.

Heck, invert the camera and put yourself in the frame too. Love the result? Send it to friends immediately with a couple of taps. Upload it to Instagram for all your followers to see. All at no additional cost. Also, take videos of any damn thing, including yourself. If you're good at it and can create a viral following on TikTok and YouTube, you can make a career out of carrying your phone around.

The preceding paragraphs were not just about photography, obviously. If you are stuck in the old analogue ways of delivering customer experience, you face a huge disadvantage. You can't be selling film photography in a world of tap-tap-done snapshooting. You also can't be doing things by snail mail only, in-person only, or requiring physical signatures only. That world is done.

Spotify now helps us choose and organize our music collections and carry them everywhere. It gets to know us better and better and keeps suggesting new songs to listen to. Contrast that to the old world of music, the one from my youth. Go to shops to look for music. Buy it on physical media like LPs, cassette tapes, or CDs. Be forced to buy whole albums, even if you only wanted one or two songs on it. Make storage space at home for your collection. Discover off-chart music only through friends or by spending hours in gigantic stores browsing through their shelves.

Netflix (and its growing array of competitors) now delivers some of the best movies and TV shows ever made, for less than the monthly cost of a movie ticket. It does this without ever needing to know you personally or show up at your house to set up its equipment. You probably installed Netflix in your home with a couple of clicks (or, if you're a certain age, your kids did it for you). You have probably never had to call or visit Netflix. You don't even know where they are.

All your customers are on smartphones. All their expectations are elevated. So what are you going to do?

Two taps on your phone and a taxi shows up at your house in a few minutes. You can see the car coming on your screen and track it in real time. Get in, get out, and the payment is handled in the background. Thank you, Uber, and various similar providers.

Another few taps and dinner shows up at your door. You can choose from hundreds of restaurants in your area, track the delivery, and pay with tip without reaching into your pocket.

Our brains are being rewired every day. Every time we do something on our devices, our expectations change subconsciously. We come to expect everything to be quick and easy. We expect food to arrive within the hour after ordering, even though it has to be cooked, packed, and delivered from miles away. We expect our local online purchases to arrive on the same or next day—a few days later is now unthinkable.

All your customers are on smartphones. All their expectations are elevated. So what are you going to do?

TOO GOOD TO IGNORE

Google Maps has more than one billion active users. Nine zeros.

I use it every day. You probably do too. It's just too damn convenient to ignore, isn't it? It maps the city out perfectly, tells you where the traffic is and which roads to avoid, estimates pretty accurate arrival times, and allows you to share your ETA with those who are waiting for you.

What's not to like?

It's not perfect, mind you. Like many things Google, it lacks a sense of taste. It's never elegant. The interface never feels like it's designed to help users who will be peering at it while rushing somewhere. And yet. Nine zeros. It beats all its competitors hands down.

How come we use it all the time, though? Consider this: If a man called Mr. Google waited for you outside your gate every morning, got into the passenger seat as you took off, and then told you which route was best for you as you drove, would you be cool with that? What if this constant companion was taking notes all the time about your destinations and interests? Hell no . . .

And yet that's what we let Google do every day. Columnist John Naughton once pointed out that we trade the usefulness and convenience of tech products against our privacy. We allow ourselves to be turned into clouds of very intimate data so that advertisers can pop up and try to coax us into buying their stuff. Most people don't seem to care. I do, and yet I keep using Google Maps. Nine zeros.

The utility and convenience of the product wins. We look away from the potential dark side, because the thing itself is just too damn useful.

I buy a lot of books from Amazon. I wish I didn't. Amazon poses a serious existential threat to something that I love deeply: physical bookshops. I don't want a world without old-fashioned bookshops in it. I want to go to them and be surprised by what I find in the rear shelves; I want to chat with people who get purpose from selling books. They're usually good, decent, old-fashioned folks, not rapacious money-grabbers. But they're dying out, because people find Amazon just too convenient.

Why do I still give Amazon my money? Because my taste in books is both too wide and too esoteric to be catered for by the average bookshop. I do buy many, many regular books (and some unusual ones) from my favorite local stores, but it is just not worth their while to stock all the offbeat titles I am usually looking for. And so I often end up at Amazon, simply because the book I want is pretty much always there.

These days, it can make its way to me pretty quickly too. And when the urgency is high, as it sometimes is with professional books, one tap and the book appears on my Kindle app in seconds . . .

So I patronize these businesses even though I am wary of them. I don't want giant corporations to know my every move and purchase and preference all the time. And yet I'm still there. Why? Because they have made themselves impossible to detach from.

If you are a businessperson, you should be very alert to this phenomenon. How easy is it to buy from you? How awkward do you make it for your busy customers to get your product? How much unnecessary time do they expend in getting to you? In this tap-tap-done world, where do you sit? Do you satisfy a need so uniquely and powerfully that they will put up with your inefficiencies?

Love them or hate them, the tech giants are making it very, very easy to become their customers (in Google's case, since we pay nothing for most of their services, we aren't even customers—we are the product being packaged and sold to advertisers, who are the real customers). There are deep lessons about user interfaces, ease of use, and sheer convenience to be had here—if we pay attention.

To give credit where it's due: My two banks have both ramped up the digital CX these days. I can do most transactions on my mobile apps. They recognize my face or thumbprint rather than needing to see me or my signature. I can approve transactions from anywhere in the world. I can make investments and monitor their returns. It's good now—but they had to be jolted into this by digital newcomers.

Most organizations need to give a lot more attention to regular customer experience and daily customer journeys. What is it like to be a user of our services? Where do the delays and irritations occur? Can we smooth them out? Can new tech reduce the frictions? Can well-spoken, helpful human beings make it all OK?

Are you even asking these questions?

THE DIGITAL CUSTOMER JOURNEY

Whether you were born digital, like Spotify and Airbnb, or became digital later, like Netflix and China's insurance giant Ping An, you absolutely have to use digital to improve the customer experience. Where to begin?

Let me take you back to the customer journey first discussed in chapter 3. You will recall that customers experience several stages in their exposure to your offering: First, they become aware of a purchase need. Next, they place you against competing alternatives. Then they move on to buy your offering, and actually use it. And finally, they mull over the experience.

Every part of this journey is an opportunity to please the customer—or inflict pain on them! Where in the journey does the pain or gain occur for the customer?

That's where digital technology comes in: It helps

you *accelerate* and *smooth* the customer journey. Digital tools make you easier to find and remove frictions along the path.

When customers are recognizing a need in their lives, how will you show up in their mind space? Do they need to observe your offerings physically, or can you reach them virtually? That's why social media and search engines have become a necessary part of the customer journey. So have user-friendly, fast-loading, easy-to-navigate corporate websites.

When they're actually buying from you, how easy will you make it for them? Can they buy what you sell online, and how many clicks or taps are needed to complete the transaction? Does it work first time, every time? Even if they show up at your place, have you invested in digital technology that showcases the inventory that's not on the premises? Is the final payment process quick and smooth?

Next, how easy is your product when they're actually utilizing it? If you're Netflix or Uber—very. If you're a bank or an insurance company, you will have to work very, very hard to make complicated transactions easy to complete on your mobile apps or online. You will have to invest in multiple technology partners; you will probably also have to shed a few as you go.

And the final part of the journey, where the customer is reflecting on the experience? That's where most providers fall asleep. A few years ago my regular insurance company did not even remember to remind me to renew a policy. They couldn't give a credible reason when I asked why. I dumped them immediately.

Today, you need to have automated renewal offers and reminders for anything that's subscription based. You also need to have kept in touch with customers, long after they last paid anything. In the old days, savvy salespeople would keep personally in touch with their key customers—they would call and visit, to show interest and concern.

These days, multiple digital tools have appeared to help you stay in touch with the customer, and to prompt them to renew and continue their business with you. The *Financial Times*, for example, has a very elegant digital product interface these days that's a pleasure to use. It regularly sends me email summaries of headline news—to keep me using the product. It invites me to in-person and virtual meetups—to tempt me to extend my usage into different formats. It shares summaries of the number of articles I read in a year, and of my interest patterns—to show me that my usage confirms how this is a valuable expense for me. And so I usually click the Renew button (which is also made very easy to do) without too much thought—despite the eye-watering price.

Impressive digital smarts for a company whose only business model until quite recently was to get printed newspapers into your hand.

Digital technology infiltrates most products and services these days. Google Analytics can help you discern behavior patterns on your website. Shopify is an all-in-one e-commerce platform that helps any business create an online store with enhanced shopping experiences. Zendesk gives you a suite of customer-support tools, including ticketing and live chat. Hootsuite helps you to manage social media presence and monitor brand sentiment. Salesforce can give you comprehensive tools for managing customer interactions, sales, and support.

This isn't just about companies whose products can be turned easily into zeros and ones. CEMEX makes and sells cement and ready-mix concrete—and has made even that digital! The multinational company launched CEMEX Go, a multi-device app that allows its customers to place orders, track deliveries, and manage invoicing and payment—without troubling a human being. Importantly, this app covers many parts of the customer journey. Once you register on a phone or tablet, you can immediately see a full array of available products and delivery locations. You can place an order with just a few taps. And you can then choose your delivery option and time it to align with your construction project timelines—a very important feature for customers in that industry.

Consider also another organization, one founded in 1932—that maker of colored plastic bricks, LEGO.

If the internet and little screens for little fingers and video games should have disrupted anyone, it would have been the famous Danish maker of the toys of yesteryear. Yet here it stands, one of the world's leading brands, with buoyant sales, opening new physical stores all over the world. What's that all about?

LEGO has seen its share of trouble. From its founding in 1932 all the way to 1998, the company never posted a loss. But by 2003 its sales were spiraling downward, and it was heavily in debt. The brick was obsolete, consultants told LEGO. The future is in diversification: jewelry, clothes, theme parks, they said—all things LEGO had no competitive advantage in. It nearly went under.

And yet, today it is called the Apple of toys. Which retailer do you know planning to open 160 new physical locations? All while its erstwhile toymaker competitors are tumbling around it. Is there a lesson here we can all learn? Yes, there is.

LEGO embraced the digital world and worked with it. It did not deny it, fear it, or ignore it. It saw that the world had shifted, and decided to move with it. It transformed from a toymaker to an architect of immersive play experiences—both physical and virtual.

To do this, the company had to engage properly with its customers. It began encouraging interaction and allowing young customers to share their creations online. It created an insights team that spends time with kids, watching them at play and noting their preferences. It looked around and saw that LEGO would not make it on its own; it had to become a partner of the hit franchises that the kids of today love. *The Lego Movie* and *The Lego Batman Movie* have been superhits. The company releases kits linked to the Marvel *Avengers* films and that allow you to make programmable robots. It has video games that require you to scan LEGO pieces. It rolled out LEGO Life, a social network for kids under the age of thirteen.

None of this assures success. The firm still hits

sales blips and sometimes has to lay off some employees. But that's par for the course in disruptive times. The point is: LEGO gets it. Do you?

The real lessons about melding old worlds with new are these:

- Stay intimately in touch with your customers.
- See how to blend old with new.
- Move on from products and channels to experiences.
- Work with partners who are central to the new world.
- Try many things, but stay true to what you're actually good at.
- Avoid distracting diversifications and misguided mergers.

Most will fall at the first hurdle. They will waste years in denial—asserting that the world they know is still strong and true, that the good old days will be back. When your market is moving on without you, you need to toss your nostalgia out the window and start studying hard data. And you need to get out of your internal echo chambers, such as your boardroom, and start watching and tracking customers—not the dying ones also invested in the past, but the ones who will be at the center of the future.

Easier said than done. Not many incumbents will pull this off; nor will many willingly undergo the wrenching changes in culture and strategy that are needed. They will get into the history books, but not the business pages of the future.

A word about my own little business. We deal mostly in in-person interactions: seminars and workshops, sounding-board sessions, off-sites, and training programs. But we too have invested in a multiplicity of digital tools: Zoom, to help deliver some experiences virtually; Mailchimp, to help manage our email list and stay in touch with clients and alumni; SurveyMonkey, to liven up our gatherings with quick-and-easy polls; Canva, to design visual content for social media; Synthesia, to generate video promos quickly and cost-effectively. And increasingly, ChatGPT in its many useful incarnations. Many more are in the offing.

No one is just analogue anymore. You can't be, in a world that went tap-tap-done years ago. Whatever you're in the business of making or selling, you need to rethink how customers experience your brand and master the latest digital tools that make connecting with you feel simpler and faster, with minimal effort on their part.

AND NOW, THE FOURTH WAVE

At the beginning of this chapter, I highlighted the three waves of computing tech that we have gone through over the past four decades or so: the personal computer, the internet, and the cloud-connected, multifeatured smartphone.

Wave 4 is now well and truly upon us. Artificial

intelligence. The world as we know it is being rewritten—not by quill and parchment, not even by keyboard and screen, but by algorithms that can teach themselves to get better. We're talking about a seismic shift in how we live, work, and play.

It's all happening so fast, that anything I write about product details and use case specifics may be obsolete by the time you read it. But let me discern the patterns of impact that are being revealed rapidly.

At the time of writing, we are entering year three of the fourth wave. AI has been a long time coming, but with its new generative versions becoming widely available, it's finally popped. This could be the most disruptive wave yet. It could make or break us. Machines are now learning, adapting, and even surpassing human capabilities.

Please note: AI comes with real risks, not just excitement. There's fear that AI, left unchecked, could go rogue, making decisions harmful to humans or being manipulated for dark purposes. Yuval Noah Harari warns that AI isn't just a *tool*—it's an *agent*, capable of outsmarting its creators if we don't stay in control. And let's not forget the looming threat to jobs. As AI automates more tasks, it's not just blue-collar work at risk but whiter collars too. CEOs must prepare for these seismic shifts or risk a wave of disruption, unrest, and deepening inequality.

Whatever lies ahead, large language models that can generate remarkable content from simple prompts in everyday language are becoming more widely available. What was once the stuff of science fiction has become very real, in no time at all. Students are conducting super-quick research and writing top-grade essays. Businesses are creating written and visual marketing content, indistinguishable from that generated by humans, fast. Musicians are composing original, innovative tracks without lifting a traditional instrument. Game designers are creating immersive environments and complex characters at a fraction of the time and money investment of yesteryear. Medical images and test results are getting analyzed and diagnosed early and more accurately, and personalized medicine is on the horizon.

This could go anywhere, but what is already clear is that AI is a massive productivity enhancer for all of us. We are individually more powerful with AI at our side. We can do so many things better and more quickly with a supercharged virtual assistant playing wingman.

But I'm not here just to tell you about robots writing sonnets. For businesses, generative AI is revolutionizing the business landscape and redefining customer journeys. Its impact is profound, offering unparalleled capabilities that enhance every touchpoint of the customer experience.

Chatbots are now at another level and can deliver first-response customer service that is far more accurate than before and even displays empathy. These bots-with-brains can work 24/7, don't get tired or irritable, can handle multiple languages, and are already sounding nearly human in their interactions. Behind the scenes in the back office, AI can automate many routine tasks such as handling inquiries, processing orders, and managing returns.

AI tools can go through megabytes of customer data and generate true personalization. They can predict with eerie precision what products are likely to appeal to specific customers. This boosts sales and loyalty. To experience this, look no further than the Netflix home page for your particular user profile. Netflix already knows you very, very well, simply by observing your consumption patterns. It will generate recommendations that will pique your interest effortlessly, with minimal human involvement.

Business content creation is also undergoing a dramatic upsurge. Blog posts, social media updates, ad copy—it's all being generated double-quick, without overwhelming marketing teams.

Dynamic pricing is something every airline and e-commerce platform is delivering at warp speed. I hate to break it to you if you didn't know this, but you aren't being quoted standard prices for those tickets and products. Market trends, competitor pricing, product availability, and customer behavior histories are being analyzed in mere moments to deliver bespoke prices that can change by the minute.

Generative AI is not just a technological advancement; it's a potentially transformative force that is reshaping the way businesses operate and interact with customers. By enhancing personalization, automating tasks, and providing deep insights, AI is creating richer, more satisfying customer journeys.

Let's consider a couple of trailblazers.

Lemonade has set the cat among the pigeons in the traditional insurance industry. The upstart company's AI chatbots—AI Maya to create personalized quotes, and AI Jim to handle claims—have set new service standards. Short ad videos deliver the company's messaging, right in the app. Everything is super simple, super quick, and that's the big differentiator. What's under the hood? A data analytics engine that quantifies risks and likely losses, and places customers in appropriate premium segments. The engaging, humanlike bots use that data to provide real-time interaction. No paperwork, no phone calls, insurance bought and claims settled in a matter of minutes. A tech-savvy new generation of customers is all in.

Spotify, aforementioned, is not just a music-streaming service; it's a musical matchmaker, curating fresh lists every week for you filled with undiscovered gems based on your listening habits. It seems to know your tastes better than you do and becomes a personalized DJ. Make no mistake about how this is happening: It's the AI. It now has more than half a billion active users and is available in almost every country in the world. When you consider that it has achieved this pitted against competitors of the size and scale of Apple, Amazon, and Google, you can only applaud. Spotify did this not just by offering more songs, but by beating the rest of the pack on CX—digital CX.

I trust you have concluded that the AI Express has left the station, and that if you haven't hopped aboard already, you risk getting left behind in a trail of digital dust. AI delivers speed and personalization, and those are at the heart of CX. You can't ignore it, any more than your forebears ignored electricity.

But wait.

In time, every business you know will use these tools. You will, but so will all your competitors. The first race is not to be left behind. Then what? The truth is, just being familiar with AI is not going to win you any prizes. To truly differentiate your CX, you need to get back to something quite ancient: the human.

HUMANIZE AS YOU DIGITIZE

We look around and see that our competitors are racing ahead with digital initiatives—to reach customers in new ways, and to achieve dramatic efficiencies in work and delivery. We feel the pressure to make a massive push in digital acceleration ourselves.

My mantra in gatherings to discuss matters digital is always the same: *Humanize as you digitize.*

But what do those words mean, and how do you do it?

The point is simple: You don't go digital without thinking about the people around the new digital—the customers and employees. Digital initiatives are primarily focused on customer benefit, and they are delivered by employees, who must also feel the benefit. If your new digital platforms are not embraced by those two groups of people, you will encounter massive resistance and friction. A bit of human-centered thinking up front will help you avoid that.

Don't roll out technological initiatives as IT projects; roll them out as human projects.

Managing the emotions around technological change matters as much as managing the server farms, security protocols, and code.

Perhaps you have an initiative in mind. *Omnichannel* is a big buzzword these days; we can run with that by way of example. Let's say you want to introduce new digital channels alongside your current ones, to sell and serve better and to expand your reach. This might involve upgrading your web presence, raising your Insta and TikTok game, or creating a smartphone-centered customer transactions portal powered by AI if you are in the B2B (business to business) game.

This is how the "humanize" part kicks in. Before you do anything, sit down and map out the human implications of the new tech. Firstly, how will customers benefit? Will they feel the need to change, or will they resist? How will you manage their expectations, hold their hands, train them in the new ways? Think about the benefits, and create a compelling narrative around it. Will customers save time or money? Will they get a better, more personal experience? Or will they just encounter delays and frustrations as they are forcibly migrated to a new system?

Next, think about employees. Will they want this, or will they hate it? Will they feel hope or just fear? Will they come on board quickly to learn and deploy, or will they passive-aggressively resist the change? Who will revel in the new tech, and who will be its victims? What new skill sets will be needed, and how will you develop them?

Lastly, what are the implications for organizational culture? Do these new ways of working lead to impacts on behavioral norms? Which part of culture do we want to shake up or discard, and what should be protected?

Intelligent leaders do not do tech in isolation; they run tech projects as human accelerations, not just digital ones. They manage customer and employee sentiment very carefully even as they introduce dramatically different ways of working. They ensure that they begin with the *why* of the change, not just the who-what-how-where details. They sell the change first, by creating a coalition of the willing.

The rest plunge in with detailed project plans and charts, as though changing a human organization can be run as an engineering project. They ignore sentiment, find it irrelevant, and trample all over it. They value secrecy over participation. And then they find themselves mired in a failing project.

No matter how much technology we deploy, we need the buy-in of humans. Humans will need to plan and deliver the change, humans will need to receive its benefits, and humans will need to work in new ways. So if you don't know how to deal with humans, you don't know how to introduce any meaningful change.

Feelings. Those old-fashioned things we had, long

before we had smartphones. They still drive behavior. They spur us on to participate or make us wallow in lethargy. They make us embrace change or recoil in uncertainty.

Are feelings part of your digital project plan?

Remember my trip to Singapore's Raffles hotel back in the day? When the family and I got back from a sightseeing trip one evening, we bumped into one of the hotel's sharply dressed, ubiquitous butlers in the corridor. This person proceeded to greet us all by name and ask how our trip to ride the Singapore Flyer went.

I stopped, puzzled. We had never met this particular butler before, much less shared details of our activities. I asked him to reveal how he seemed to know so much about us. He grinned and reluctantly showed me his iPad, a new gadget in those days. All butlers could access names and photos of all current guests and were encouraged to memorize as many as possible. He had simply looked up our details when seeing us approaching from the other end of the corridor and knew that we had booked an excursion to the Flyer that day. Simple. And so clever.

That was in 2011, when smartphones and tablets were still very new. But the Raffles team was ahead of the game, deploying hardware and software not only for their own sake but to elevate the very human aspects of guest interaction. Greetings, conversations, and offers to be of assistance.

Machine and human combined, to produce world-class CX.

Here's another example of machine and human working together. Do you know of the Folio Society? Unless you're a bibliophile, you probably don't. They create beautiful special editions of classic books. Books done the old-fashioned way: in hardcover, usually cloth-bound; with premium paper and elegant typography; and given a new twist by specially commissioned illustrators.

A book lover's delight. But expensive. Surely that's a tiny market in today's age, those folks willing to pay even more for books to keep as collectibles or give out as gifts?

Feelings. Those old-fashioned things we had, long before we had smartphones. They still drive behavior.

Actually, the market exists. There are billions of humans out there, and the trick is to find the minimum viable market that makes even esoteric ventures worthwhile. The digital era makes this possible.

That's where modern tools and tricks come in. The

Folio Society was founded in 1947 in London. To stay viable today, it needs to address a bigger global market. And so I was delighted to see this old-fashioned book-loving enterprise on Instagram, highlighting its splendid editions of timeless literature. I was also very happy to see a summer sale being announced—lots of books at half the normal price.

I jumped in immediately. These books are not routinely affordable, so one must make the most of the opportunity to get them for less. I clicked through to an elegant website, nicely rendered on my phone browser, found three books of interest, added them to my cart, and tried to pay and check out.

That's where the trouble began.

The website seemed to have a problem reconciling my preferred delivery address with my credit card's billing address. I tried using PayPal instead—similar issues. The site would not flag the problem; the transaction would simply stall. After thirty minutes of trying various options, I gave up. Life is short. Oh well.

But a rescue operation was in progress. A day later, I received an email, no doubt automated, that I had items in my cart and had not checked them out. Was I interested in trying again? it asked. Just click here . . . I was impressed, so decided to give it another shot. This time I clicked through on my laptop, hoping the site's payments engine would be more robust on the bigger screen.

Sadly not. I hit the same transaction-completion problems as before after wasting even more time. Annoyed, I fired off a complaint and left it at that.

But that, too, was not the end. I received a very courteous and apologetic email (from a real person, this time), expressing regret and asking if I was available for a phone call in which everything would be resolved. Now, I hate doing things on the phone, and in any case I would hesitate to provide card details in that way. I said so.

The lady on the other end would not give up, though. She asked if she could call me at a time of my convenience and promised me the transaction would be secure, taking very little time. I gave in and sent her my number and a time. She called on the button; she was friendly to a fault, and the deed was indeed done in just a few minutes.

I got the books; they got their money.

Great CX in the digital era is indeed about new technologies, fresh channels, quick transactions, and short interactions. But it is also about people. Folio had a great human in play, to rescue the situation from a CX fail to a CX win. They no doubt need to work on their online payment systems for the global customer (human rescue would be prohibitively expensive if it became too frequent). Nonetheless this organization knows something essential about customer care: The people interface matters just as much. The future is both analogue and digital.

Two things won the day for them. First, if the product is truly distinctive and can't be obtained elsewhere, customers will probably hang in there and be forgiving. If not, they will leave in a click and get what they want elsewhere. Second, if key people are engaged with their work and proud of it, they will rescue many situations for you, with warmth and empathy.

If you have neither distinctive products nor distinctive people, then even the best digital tools can't save you.

7 Jazz It

Always be a first-rate version of yourself, instead of a second-rate version of somebody else.

—Judy Garland

Benchmarking.

A sophisticated word, no? It's what the business world uses to describe being as good as the best. When you are benchmarked, you are right up there with the market leaders.

Or are you?

We are constantly peering over fences and into windows. The lives of others fascinate us. We have a lifelong obsession with knowing what they are doing, how they do it, and what we need to copy from them.

This is the noise in our heads:

What are they wearing? Where do they get that

stuff? How do they look so effortlessly stylish? I feel shabby now. I wonder what that ensemble costs? Where are their kids schooling? Where do they get that kind of money? I wonder what their secret is? Let me keep looking, so I can figure it out . . .

Way too many of us spend entire lifetimes gaping over the fence at the neighbor's garden, wondering why the grass is always greener on the other side. We do this both literally and metaphorically: in our gardens but also in our businesses, social circles, and clubs. *Why do they look better than us?*

What do we think we will learn from all this obsessive gazing? Perhaps the secrets of our neighbors, so we can replicate their success. Perhaps a few tips. Perhaps we just gawk in sheer envy, fixated by the sight because our own lives seem so drab and dreary in comparison.

In business this practice has respectable names: benchmarking, competitor analysis, market intelligence. We pay for this stuff. We hire people and go to business school to help us compare ourselves and to learn from the best. We believe it helps.

We forget that those we are benchmarking against never benchmarked themselves against anyone and that they never seem to bother to gather any intelligence about us . . .

And that right there is the point. That's why the grass is always greener on the other side: because your neighbors never waste any time peering at your garden. If their grass is greener, it's because they tend to it better. They know what matters.

In my experience, individuals and business leaders who make it big the right way—through innovation, application, and determination—have something in common: They really aren't bothered by what others are doing. They form their own ideas, clarify them over time through trial and error, and keep going, resolutely, even in adversity.

The rest? Well, they keep peering at everyone else, wondering what the "secret" is. Here's your answer, voyeurs: that grass didn't grow itself. Someone thought about the grass, chose it, planted it, nurtured it, and gave it time and attention. As opposed to what you're doing.

I am always bemused when I do some work with companies that win the "Best Organization to Work For" award. I usually find that their own employees are generally amazed they won such an award, are ready to bitch and twitch about their bosses as much as anyone else, and half of them have their CVs ready if the chance to move arises. And yet employees in competing firms look at the award winner with envy, thinking it must be idyllic to work there.

Benchmarking is the business world's sophisticated form of mimicry and copy-pasting. It's hailed as a tool for achieving excellence, but often it's just a siren call that will lead your company into the dull waters of mediocrity. It seems like a smart play: Let's learn and use the practices of top performers and try to replicate them to catapult our own performance. But the kicker is this: It usually weakens those who do it.

What happens when you are a CEO telling your

people you have to copy someone else? You have actually admitted defeat. *They are better than us,* you have declared, *and we must catch up in desperation.* Benchmarking is imitation, not innovation. Eventually we have a business landscape littered with copycats, all trying to outdo each other by using the exact same playbook. It's a recipe for sameness, not distinction.

A SEA OF SAMENESS

When I was young, cars all looked different. The first car I ever drove was a Datsun 120Y—my mother's—and it had a cutely weird boxy shape. It could not be mistaken for any other car. Similar Japanese makes—Toyota, Honda, Mazda—all had distinctive shapes and styling.

In those days, a Peugeot looked distinctively like a Peugeot, a Mercedes could be spotted from a mile away, a Volvo could not be mistaken for any other car, a Citroën was its own thing, and a Jaguar was distinction epitomized. Their designers celebrated being different.

What on earth happened? Look at new cars today and you see the sea of sameness that surrounds us. After a couple of decades of copying and mimicry, bland conformity rules the roost. Every mainstream model seems to be trying to look like every other mainstream model.

Walking through a suburban street in London on my travels recently, I passed by a parked midsize SUV.

It looked a little dull, a little meh. I happened to notice the logo and was astonished it was an MG. An MG—that beautiful little roadster, reduced to suburban conformity? And lo and behold, down the street I walked past near-identical Honda, Hyundai, and Jaguar SUV models—and looking at them from the side, I was unable to name the makes.

Alex Murrell, a digital marketing strategist, calls our current epoch the "Age of Average." This problem is not confined to cars. Mr. Murrell points out that most recently furnished Airbnb apartments look insipidly familiar, most modern city centers have the same array of glassy skyscrapers, and there is a particular "Instagram face" look that social media influencers are driving young women toward.

In publishing, once there was a best-selling self-help book with a four-letter swear word in the title, a whole bunch of imitators using the same word were soon on the shelves.

In my observation, businesses and business leaders are also notable mostly for their similarities, not their differences. Most of the players in an industry offer the exact same products, their offices are furnished virtually identically, they jive in the same jargon and patter in the same patois in their boardrooms, they think the same thoughts, and their so-called strategies are interchangeable.

This is so dispiriting. Instead of reveling in difference, we are sinking into sameness. Why do we do it? One reason is that humans are natural mimics—we look around and learn from others, and eventually this drives us into uniformity. It also happens because designers and manufacturers who are constrained by the need for short-term hits inevitably play safe—they go with what sells easily, not what stands out.

Yes, efficiency and uniformity are comfortable, but why do we just want to be comfortable? Why do we—parents, teachers, leaders—persist in telling everyone to look and sound and be the same? That cloak of sameness is not a comfortable fit; it is a straitjacket.

As a strategist, I have to tell you that the minute you take everyone down the path of sameness, you are striving for only one thing: mediocrity. Think about it this way: The thing that's being copied, who came up with it? There was an original mind, individual or collective, that went for it—that look, that style, that process, that idea—and when it succeeded, a huge crowd of copiers followed. The originator set the trend and the standard; the mimics lacked the guts and savvy to be original, so they just . . . copied.

Who has the real achievement?

Yes, humanity transmits its best ideas, and humanity adopts quickly and at scale. But is that where true success sits? Rather than lead people into bland conformity, a thoughtful leader rails for distinction.

Let's pause here to consider what seems like a paradox. Aren't some of our most noted companies actually "fast followers"? Isn't Apple, for example, usually slow off the mark in innovation, and doesn't it mostly introduce products and features that have long been in the market?

Yes, it does. Apple was not the first to come up

with an icon-driven computer operating system. It did not introduce the first MP3 music player, and it was late into smartphones and tablets. There were many smartwatches and headphones in the market before Apple ever emerged with its own versions. And new features that get headlined in iOS upgrades for the iPhone have often been available for Android for months and years.

Remember this: If everyone's zigging, they are following someone who zagged.

So isn't Apple just benchmarking?

No, there's a subtle difference. Innovation is not about being the first to market; it's about being the *best* to market. Apple tends to bring its legendary ease of use and intuitive user interfaces into play when it launches anything. The iPod was the first hugely popular music player because it was trivially easy to use and trailblazed the ability to buy digital music cheaply. The Apple Watch may have been late to the market, but it quickly became the world's most popular watch brand because of its simple sophistication. Apple's AirPods were similarly late, but their seamless integration with the Apple ecosystem made them a massive success. In 2023 alone Apple was estimated to have sold seventy-five million AirPods.

This isn't benchmarking; it's waiting to do things right.

If you're a CEO, push your people toward difference. Make them highlight what's special and unique in your offerings, not just what benchmarks well. This is not to seek difference for its own sake, mind you, but a meaningful divergence from the crowd. What makes you stand out with customers? What makes your employee experience different from everything else out there? If your customer encountered five product experiences in a day, would yours be the one that stood out—or the one that was forgotten in the crowd of clones?

If you're the leader of difference, you'd better be the one who embraces diversity of thought and encourages debate and dissent. If you're the one who encourages everyone to look the same and do what's safe, then you will win the prize for passability.

Remember this: If everyone's zigging, they are following someone who zagged.

JAZZ THE CX

Everything I've written in this chapter so far applies to customer experience.

It's a thing businesses do, to observe the CX other

businesses offer. To send mystery shoppers to check out the competition. To gaze over the fence to see why the grass is greener.

Gaze away, by all means. But don't use the intel you gather to copy; use it to stand out.

Great CX is jazz; it's not a symphony. It's improv, not scripted sameness. There are no correct notes everyone has to follow. Great CX demands the fluidity and responsiveness of jazz.

In jazz, musicians riff off each other, improvising in the moment, adapting to the flow of the music and the energy of the audience. They're not following a preset script; they're creating something new and unique in real time. This is exactly what great customer experience entails—improvisation, creativity, and a deep understanding of the current moment and context.

If you try to benchmark someone else's jazz, it will be like trying to replicate a Miles Davis solo note for note. You might get the technicalities right, but you will drain the life out of the performance. You will miss out on the soul, the spontaneity—the very things that made it extraordinary in the first place.

Customers are dynamic; their needs and preferences are constantly evolving. To truly excel in customer experience, you need to be in tune with these shifts, ready to adapt and improvise. This means listening actively, responding intuitively, and sometimes taking risks. It's about creating those unexpected moments of delight that a rigid, benchmarked approach simply can't produce.

Let's pause again.

Much of the best CX is also system-and-process driven. That part, by definition, is structured and predictable. Response times have to be within preset parameters; the responses themselves can't be whimsical and all over the place. Excellent CX also demands rigorous processes and consistent execution. Where's the jazz in that?

Actually, the best customer experiences are those that harmonize both elements, much like a jazz musician who improvises within the framework of a well-rehearsed tune.

In the world of customer experience, systems and processes are crucial—they ensure reliability, efficiency, and a baseline of quality service. These frameworks are akin to the underlying structure of a jazz composition, providing the foundation upon which improvisation can occur. The jazz in customer experience emerges when businesses empower their employees to go beyond the script, to read the nuances of customer interactions, and to deliver personalized, memorable experiences. It's about having the flexibility to adapt and innovate within the established framework, creating moments of magic that a rigid, formulaic approach could never achieve.

This is what I mean when I ask you to "jazz the CX." Sure, have the structure of systematic processes, but also have the freedom to improvise. A robust foundation will ensure consistency and reliability, but a culture where employees are encouraged to think creatively and respond intuitively to customer needs is also a winning play. This dynamic interplay between structure and spontaneity is what transforms good customer service into *great* customer experience—turning every interaction into a unique performance that resonates deeply with customers.

Now, let's meet the jazz players. Let's take a closer look at some of the best organizations out there that are landing their CX in fresh and original ways.

BANKING BY HUMANS

When I was a young professional working in London, a brand-new bank popped up. It was called First Direct, and it was very different. No branches, just telephone banking. It gave you a checkbook and a debit card, and that was it. But you could call the folks there 24/7. This was a fintech before fintechs were a thing, and I loved the CX. Helpful, knowledgeable bankers, available any time of day or night? It suited me perfectly, and I embraced it enthusiastically.

Decades later, First Direct is still thriving. Now, of course, you interact with the bank not just by phone but by using internet and mobile channels as well. But here's the thing: First Direct humanized as it digitized. It is committed to immediate human interaction. Other banks use automated phone trees and voice recognition systems; First Direct tries to ensure that every call is answered quickly, by an actual human being.

It also doesn't have a separate CX team; the whole bank is about CX. All employees, from frontline warriors in the trenches with customers to senior executives conducting the jazz players, are aligned to delivering standout CX. Indeed, the bank even recruits staff from the caring professions like health care and hospitality, to inject empathy into its customer interactions.

Current CEO Chris Pitt emphasizes four values: Stand together, bring a smile, make things better, and give a shit.

Refreshingly different!

Stefan Stern, writing in the *Financial Times*, explained how those values play out in practice. Staff are given autonomy, with no scripts to stick to, and no average handling times measured on calls. Since COVID-19 lockdown, employees are free to work at home or in the office, whichever suits them best. Customer calls are always answered by a human being, not a bot. And dozens of staff have been deployed to advise specifically on areas like financial vulnerability and domestic violence.

Two instruments, humans and technology, being played with creativity to produce a jazz score. First Direct regularly tops all industry customer service league tables, including being named as the most highly rated organization for customer satisfaction across *all* UK sectors and industries in 2021.

IMPROV IN THE SKIES

Let's take off now with another jazz player, Southwest Airlines. From the get-go, Southwest has been focused on fun—for employees and passengers. Why fun? Because we are at our best when we are smiling and laughing. Southwest's famously humorous and creative passenger safety announcements on their aircraft often go viral. Why is this great CX? Because when you have laughed thanks to a business, you are already predisposed to be generous toward it.

Southwest's CX is not just about improv and stand-up comedy, of course. It offers the full gamut of customer support channels, including phone, live chat via mobile app, and an extensive self-help resource center, plus recent improvements, such as real-time travel communications and simplified flight-change processes.

Who makes great CX for Southwest? The employees. They are given class-leading benefits such as generous pension contributions, profit sharing, stock-purchase options, and quality health plans that include vision and dental. Those who stick with the company get lifelong professional development via training and mentorship.

Do the folks at Southwest follow all the CX practices outlined in this book? Well, they boss it—customer satisfaction is embedded right up there in the mission statement. They humanize it, by nurturing an engaged workforce that cares about customers naturally. And they certainly jazz it, simply by putting fun and laughter in their playbook.

Digital is where they fell short in 2022, when a stinging setback caused by outdated software caused a billion-dollar meltdown. That's why working on all four CX practices in tandem is so important. Three ticks out of four also won't cut it in these demanding times.

YOU DECIDE WHAT'S BEST

Let's bring the jazz ensemble back to Earth again, by considering a business that sells rather mundane, old-world services: shoe repair, key cutting, and lock mending. Timpson is a family-owned business in the UK, on the main shopping streets since 1865. It should probably have died out decades ago, but here it is, still going strong, with more than two thousand branches and nearly six thousand employees.

Timpson could well have gone under in the 1980s, until John Timpson had an epiphany: that success would depend on the way customers were served—and that success depended most critically on the employees in the branches, and their relationships with customers. Timpson calls this "upside-down management."

The company went for a three-pronged approach: First, recruit naturally friendly people to work in its stores; second, give them a large degree of freedom to decide what is best for their customers; and third, support them in every possible way to do their best work.

Simple common sense—which isn't that common!

Here's what Timpson doesn't do. It doesn't do formal recruitment tests. Selection panels measure candidates off an informal scale that emphasizes character, friendliness, readiness to smile, natural energy. It doesn't have rigid price lists—store managers can give discounts if they deem them appropriate. It doesn't have national promotions—stores can decide what should be highlighted in their local markets.

More jazz: Store managers get an allowance to be

used to settle complaints. Managers are not overlords who issue orders; they are coaches who support the rest. The performance review system is centered on a "Happy Index"—you just rate the degree of support you received from key people who are meant to aid you. A simple weekly bonus is shared by all employees in a store.

Timpson is also renowned for its social responsibility initiatives, notably its commitment to hiring ex-offenders. This policy not only provides second chances but also builds a dedicated and grateful workforce. Timpson's support for local initiatives and charities further cements its reputation as a business that genuinely cares about its community.

You're probably skeptical that the business you work for can ever do anything like what Timpson pulls off so easily. You're right to be. Most businesses are run by stay-the-course, conformist leaders; they exercise rigid control from national HQ and exist in a state of perpetual mistrust of their employees.

Timpson's brand of originality and maverick thinking takes great courage, from the board down. Timpson is bossing it in special ways and humanizing it in even more special ways. The CX jazz it plays comes from putting the human into the music.

TASTE FIRST, MONEY LATER

An episode of *Street Food: Asia* on Netflix recently caught my attention. Set in Delhi, it featured a father's simple but brilliant advice. Dalchand, who runs a bustling food stall in the heart of the city, recounted how his grandfather had started the business. His father then mastered the art of making *chaat*—a spicy, flavorful street snack—by watching his own father. That expertise was passed down to Dalchand.

Dalchand's father had one key piece of advice: *Focus on the taste. Forget the money for now,* he'd say, *just make sure the food tastes outstanding. Get that right and the rest will follow. People will come back for the taste. Reputation will grow. Profit will come. Growth will happen.*

It's simple advice—but spot-on.

Let's break it down. Focusing on taste for Dalchand means hand-picking the freshest ingredients every day. No compromises. He personally selects the produce, moving from vendor to vendor until he's satisfied. He knows the spices are crucial, too, and gets them freshly ground daily. The dish is then prepared carefully, without rushing.

The result? His costs per dish are higher, and his profit margins slimmer. But while competitors cut corners—using cheaper ingredients, prepackaged spices, or rushing the cooking process—Dalchand nails the one thing that truly matters: the taste. And that's why customers keep coming back. They're not interested in alternatives down the street. They want his chaat.

This lesson goes well beyond food. What Dalchand's father taught him echoes a key idea I wrote about in *The Bigger Deal*: Every business has one thing it must get right. For a restaurant, it's taste. Sure, good service, ambience, and convenience are great, but they're add-ons. The core is the food. Without nailing that, the rest falls flat.

When you've mastered your core, the temptation will be to scale, expand, and grow fast. But here's the tricky part: Can you grow without losing the very thing that made you special? Often, businesses can't. As they grow, they lose the meticulous attention to detail that created their success in the first place. The process becomes harder to replicate, and the magic gets diluted.

The CX lesson here is crystal clear: Know what's most important to your customer, and never compromise on that. If you nail what matters, the rest will often take care of itself.

Dalchand shows us that growth and scale aren't always the end goals. Staying small and deep, focusing on craft and quality, can be equally rewarding—both financially and in terms of personal satisfaction. Success isn't just about profits, balance sheets, or status symbols; it's also about being exceptional at what you do, earning a decent living, and keeping your peace of mind. And in the end, your customers will likely reward you for it, handsomely.

YOUR WAY, NOT THE HIGHWAY

"Be yourself; everyone else is already taken," advised Oscar Wilde.

The examples of unusual CX in the preceding sections of this chapter are not meant to give you something else to copy, I hasten to add. I hope they will inspire you to look for unique ways of doing your own CX, for the specific needs of your customers.

What have I told you about jazzing up your CX? Let's recap:

- **CX needs both structure and improv.** Robust systems, processes, and standards remain key. Efficiency and reliability matter, and that takes discipline. But always give your employees the power to improvise. Humans love to be surprised and to feel the empathy of others. Don't stifle that in your people.
- **Personalization is key.** Let staff go beyond the script. Let them decide how to be memorable and meaningful in their customers' minds. Encourage them to know their customers, quirks and all. Use human empathy as well as data to figure customers out.
- **Adaptability is essential.** Stay in tune with the dynamic flow of customer preferences. Don't be rigid. Let the music play in response to the energy and temperament of its audience. Don't turn headquarters into a dictatorship.
- **Inspire creativity.** Have the courage to be an original—it's the only long-term play that wins. Generate and lead innovation and fresh thinking in your people.

> Trust them to know what CX is best, and
> let them shape it.

We are all given a life, and there is plenty in a life to preoccupy us wholly. We have to build skills, develop expertise, gain wisdom, provide for others, and avoid pitfalls. How on earth are you going to do all that in the throes of a morbid obsession with what others are doing?

It's the same in a business. The grass can be greener on your side, too, and that's where your first attention should go. You have your garden right there under your feet. Pay attention to it, tend to it, give it nourishment, try something different. It will grow beautifully, without you ever needing to walk to the fence. The answer is on your side, not the other side.

8 CX Wisdoms

Customer experience is the new marketing.
—Steve Cannon, former CEO, Mercedes-Benz USA

I have been a student of customer experience for decades. I observe and advise, note and write, partake and reflect. I celebrate great CX wherever I find it, and I am its victim—as we all are—when it is poor.

This chapter gathers some of the deeper insights that have been generated in this journey. Some have come from me, some from others.

LISTEN TO THE RIVER

If you want to catch fish, say the Irish, listen to the sound of the river.

To understand what that means, let's first consider

how Deliveroo, the most successful food delivery app in the UK, was founded.

Deliveroo's cofounder is Will Shu, who has told his origin story in many interviews. In 2013 he was a time-stressed investment banker fed up with eating low-quality ready-to-eat meals from supermarkets. He wondered why London's huge number of excellent restaurants didn't bother to deliver food. Shu started Deliveroo by establishing a fleet of delivery riders who would take the pain out of food delivery for restaurants and diners.

Here's what he first did, though: He made himself the first rider and delivered food every day for months and months—alongside running the business!

Shu knew what he was doing. He was listening to the sound of the river, personally and intimately. He wanted to know what his customers and riders would go through before he scaled up and invested in systems and logistics. And he still completes deliveries today. He terms this practice "primary research"—doing the basic work of the enterprise, talking to customers and merchants, seeing everything firsthand. This gives him the "truest experience" of how the business actually works.

That is exactly what the best business leaders do. They boss it from day one, and make sure they listen and keep listening to every sound in their workplace and marketplace.

In 2023 Deliveroo delivered £2 billion in revenues, working in ten countries and handling seven million users and nearly three hundred million orders.

Sam Walton, who would one day be crowned the

richest person on the planet, also listened to the river. When he first got started decades ago in small-town America, he ran the same little store for seven years straight before even thinking about opening another. It wasn't because he wasn't hungry for more—it was because he knew retail is a game of patience. You've got to understand how customers tick, figure out how to move products efficiently, and get a handle on managing cash. Only when you've mastered the basics can you start to think big.

What was Walton doing in those years of staying small? The answer is simple: He was learning the business. He was serving and observing customers, and studying their needs and behavior patterns. He was understanding supply logistics. He was watching how his cash flow behaved at different times of the month. In short, he was taking his time to get it right.

People often assumed Walmart was built on some lightning-bolt idea, a quick ticket to success. Walton would just smile and remind them: Most "overnight successes" take a couple of decades to happen!

When Uber CEO Dara Khosrowshahi became worried by the frequency of complaints from his drivers, he became one himself, doing what they do, from signing up to driving customers around. He learned about the impact of traffic conditions on driver earnings, and where the app needed to be better. His personal undercover operation revealed problems that might have stayed unobserved from headquarters.

Those rare CEOs who sit at the reception desk, receiving visitors. Who roll up their sleeves to work with frontline employees. Who spend time in stores and branches to sell things. Who sit in contact centers, fielding calls, queries, and complaints. Why do they do it? That stuff is nowhere in their job descriptions.

They do it because the river is where the action is, and where its sounds must be heard. You can't be on the top floor of the main office and expect to hear anything meaningful. You will only receive muffled sounds and filtered reports up there.

That's why it's a requirement on Fast Forward, the leadership program that I founded, that every participant must commit to listening to the sound of the river, personally. They must get down on the ground and move about; they must meet and listen to frontline workers and random customers; they must do the work their people do. And they must do this frequently and regularly. Not performatively, not for the cameras, but as a sincere habit.

Both the employee experience and the customer experience become better when leaders patrol the river and listen to its sounds. It is a great investment in time, and the best leaders do this routinely.

MAKE YOURSELF A HABIT

Think about the businesses you patronize and the things you buy regularly as a customer. Your bank, your smartphone, your toothpaste, your internet provider, your skin-care routine, your airline. For how long have you stuck with certain brands and offerings?

Strategy thought leader Roger Martin observes that we tend to repeat buy routinely, but it's not always a rational or emotional reason that generates customers' loyalty and keeps them coming back—more often, it's *habit*. Customers tend to develop purchasing routines based on familiarity and convenience, not because they feel a deep emotional connection to the brand. For instance, people might repeatedly buy the same product, like Pears soap or a Samsung phone, simply because it fits into their daily habits and offers a level of familiarity, comfort, and reliability.

What really drives repeat business isn't some sentimental bond or rational calculation, but habit—plain and simple. People tend to buy the same products not because they adore the brand but because it's what they're used to. It's about convenience and routine. For example, you're more likely to keep grabbing that same brand of toothpaste because it's familiar, not because you've pledged eternal allegiance to it. Businesses that rely on customers' ingrained habits are the ones winning the day, not necessarily those focusing on constantly rebooting brand loyalty.

So what does that mean for companies? Instead of bending over backward to create undying loyalty with bells and whistles, they should be focusing on reinforcing those purchasing habits. Disrupting an already established pattern with too many changes can actually backfire, sending customers in search of something simpler. The real challenge is to keep things predictable and convenient, not constantly rebranding or tweaking your product in the name of innovation.

People like what they know. Smart businesses keep it simple and make sure their products blend seamlessly into a customer's routine without needing to be reconsidered every time.

If you want your product to become a habit-buy, the secret is to make it indispensable to a customer's daily life. It's all about ease of use, reliability, and consistent quality. Think of companies like Amazon with its one-click buying or Starbucks with its app that makes grabbing your morning coffee frictionless. These businesses are masters at fitting into the daily grind with minimal fuss. Adding in loyalty programs or perks just sweetens the deal, subtly reinforcing that habit. The goal isn't to wow people with over-the-top features but to offer a simple, reliable experience that makes sticking with your product the easiest choice every time.

So, rather than trying to dazzle customers with flashy features or dramatic overhauls, businesses should ensure their offerings blend effortlessly into the customer's life, providing a predictable and reliable experience that patrons will naturally gravitate toward again and again.

Remember: Our minds are overworked. Much of the time, we don't want new information. We don't want to rethink. We don't want to be challenged. We just want to continue with our daily set of habits. Products and CX that do just that are very valuable to us, even if that feeling is unvoiced.

So is this a reason for brands and CX leaders to be lazy and take customers for granted? Not at all.

First, we should be designing for habit—our CX should be making it easy for customers to stick to using our products. That means removing frictions in their journeys with us; it means not making dramatic changes that cause them to become unsettled. It means sticking to simple communications, and not asking the customer to do any extra work just to understand us.

Second, we must understand that even habit-bound customers can still leave us. They may be hard to shake, but when they finally leave, it's not because of minor inconveniences—it takes a major blowout. A significant disappointment, like a glaring quality failure, a terrible customer service experience, or a big disruption in their routine, is what snaps them out of the habit loop. Think about when a once-reliable product suddenly tanks or a service you counted on drops the ball spectacularly—those are the moments when even the most loyal, habit-driven customers decide enough is enough. One really bad experience can be the tipping point, or a series of annoying and disappointing missteps can be what causes irreversible damage. Once the trust is broken, it's hard to get it back. Our task then is to never get there. Let's not let our customers down so egregiously that we break the habits of a lifetime.

Lastly, we must guide our habit-bound customers during any necessarily disruptive transitions. Netflix once had customers very used to mail-delivered DVDs, but it knew it had to carry those customers across to the world of broadband streaming instead. It did this by trying to make the shift gradual, intuitive, and relatively painless. The key was offering streaming as an added benefit rather than an immediate replacement, allowing customers to explore and get comfortable with the new format on their own terms. Netflix launched its streaming service in 2007, while keeping its DVD rental service in place, giving customers time to adopt the new technology without feeling pressured.

Netflix's strategy centered on removing friction and increasing convenience. As internet speeds improved and more content became available, Netflix made it easier for users to stream content on a wide range of devices, from smart TVs to gaming consoles and smartphones. It kept the interface simple, letting customers effortlessly switch from DVDs to digital without needing to learn anything new. The instant gratification of streaming, combined with the recommendation algorithms that made discovery seamless, eventually led to a natural migration. Customers who might have initially stuck to DVDs found themselves streaming more and more because it just felt easier and more enjoyable.

The company also incentivized the switch by focusing on original content that was only available via streaming, like *House of Cards* in 2013, which gave subscribers a compelling reason to fully embrace the new model. Rather than forcing a switch, Netflix allowed customers to evolve their habits slowly until streaming became the dominant way to consume entertainment.

But wait: This process was not without its hitches.

In 2011 Netflix tried to accelerate the migration and announced that it would separate its DVD and streaming services, charging separately for each. This led to customer backlash, as the price increase was seen as sudden and unwelcome. Netflix lost around eight hundred thousand subscribers following this announcement, highlighting how difficult it was to manage the shift. To its credit, the company rapidly backtracked and withdrew the split, and CEO Reed Hastings made a public apology.

Ultimately, Netflix didn't yank its DVD service right away; instead, it gradually de-emphasized it as streaming became the habit for its customers, only fully phasing out the DVD model once the bulk of its user base had made the leap themselves.

It understood the power of habit in customer loyalty.

The question for all of us is this: Does our CX reinforce customer habits by being easy and familiar, rather than complicated and disturbing?

DON'T DELIGHT YOUR CUSTOMERS

Customer delight. Those two words have been placed together for so long that the idea now sounds like a sugary dessert. Deeper thinkers are now beginning to ask whether we should even try to deliver delight.

Matthew Dixon, Nick Toman, and Rick DeLisi lead the charge in their thought-provoking book, *The Effortless Experience.*

Dixon et al. flip the conventional wisdom about customer service on its head. They argue that businesses shouldn't be obsessed with delighting customers at every turn—because, as it turns out, delight doesn't drive loyalty the way we think it does. Instead, what really keeps customers coming back is reducing the effort they need to put in to resolve their issues. In other words, it's not about surprising or wowing customers, it's about making their interactions as smooth, simple, and frictionless as possible.

The authors make a compelling case: When customers have to jump through hoops—whether it's being transferred between departments, repeating their issue, or navigating complex processes—they are more likely to churn. Conversely, when businesses focus on making customer service effortless, customers tend to stick around. The key insight here is that most customers aren't looking for over-the-top service; they just want quick, easy solutions to their problems. For businesses, this means rethinking their strategies. Rather than aiming for moments of "delight," they should focus on minimizing frustration and reducing the time and energy customers need to invest in resolving issues. This shift from delight to simplicity is where businesses can make a real impact on loyalty and retention.

The essential proposition is this: The real win in customer experience is to mitigate disloyalty by reducing customer effort. Focusing on delights can only be occasional at best, like wonder goals scored on the soccer field. Those are lovely to behold and stay in the mind, but a team does not win by trying to deliver wows all the time. It wins by making its natural state more efficient: completed passes, tackles won, shots blocked. A high level of performance on those stats won't win any of your players the Ballon d'Or, but they might be more likely to indicate a team that can keep winning.

By paying deep attention to the various burdens we place on our customers, we can smooth out the customer journeys we offer and keep engagement high—not through superficial and short-lived delights but via the more powerful lever of making ourselves easy to deal with.

"It just works" is strong glue!

WAIT TO GET IT RIGHT

AutoXpress is a very successful motor services firm, operating across East Africa. It now offers a wide range of products and services, but a decade ago it was focused mainly on selling and installing tires. It stood out for customer service, though, and its footprint was growing rapidly. I asked the directors at the time: Your customers trust you, so why don't you move into full vehicle servicing?

Nope, they said. *Not yet.*

Servicing means spare parts, and that requires inventory for a vast range of popular vehicle makes. It also means having a team of skilled mechanics in every branch. So until we have systems *and* processes *and* skills just right, they told me, we won't make our move.

Now that's unusual. Most businesses I have observed can't wait to add new products and offerings with which to entice their captive customers. But what were AutoXpress's founders being super-protective of? The high-level customer experience they had painstakingly built over many years. It worked well for tires; it needed to be just the same for anything new. They restrained their ambitions—and their bottom line—until they were ready.

Today, the company can call itself a trusted vehicle doctor, tending to a wide range of vehicle inspections and services, and stocking a broad spectrum of parts and accessories. It has a young, enthusiastic team in every branch and efficient parts warehousing and logistics.

Great CX is a story of many moving parts, and AutoXpress's leading lights knew this. Most impressively, they knew CX was at the heart of their competitive advantage, and they weren't going to degrade it by growing in scale or scope too quickly. They retained their customers' trust, but also won the confidence of top global auto brands.

By doing CX patiently.

WHAT IS YOUR CUSTOMER REALLY BUYING?

If you sell something (and let's face it, most of us do), here's a game-changing insight:

"People don't want to buy a quarter-inch drill. They want a quarter-inch hole."

That line's been around for a while—Harvard professor Clayton Christensen attributed it to Theodore Levitt, and some say it originally came from Leo McGivena. No matter who it's from, pay close attention to what it's saying.

No one needs a drill in their life. They need what the drill does: It makes holes. But I think that insight doesn't go far enough. No one's thrilled about having holes in their walls for the sake of holes. It's about what those holes support—maybe a shelf. And even that's just another step. No one wants a shelf for the shelf's sake; it's there to showcase something that gives them a feeling. Maybe it's status, maybe it's personal pride. So it's not the drill, or the hole, or the shelf—it's the emotion behind all of it.

Here's the real kicker: People don't buy products or services. They buy feelings.

I introduced that idea in earlier chapters. Let's riff on it a little more now.

Years ago, I told my friends at Toyota in Kenya: That young woman walking into your showroom isn't looking for a car—she's there to buy the dignity or freedom that comes from escaping public transport. She's there for self-worth, for progress. That older guy checking out your luxury 4x4? He's not buying wheels—he's buying status, a signal to the world that he's made it. Same showroom, two buyers, but entirely different feelings being chased. The biggest mistake you can make is trying to sell a *car* to someone who came looking to buy *feelings*. Smart businesses, like Toyota, understand this well. They changed up the

CX in the showroom and beyond to accommodate the selling of feelings.

No one buys insurance for the paperwork. People buy peace of mind. No one buys a football shirt to stay warm—they're buying belonging, a badge of loyalty. In my own profession, I'm not selling books or advice. What people are really buying is hope—the hope of their own success and advancement. That's the actual transaction. If my books or courses don't help people move forward in life, I've failed.

Here's the real kicker: People don't buy products or services. They buy feelings.

The most successful companies have always known this. Coca-Cola's never just sold soda. East African Breweries is not selling alcohol. Apple? The iPhone was never just a phone. They're all selling feelings. Human beings don't buy functionality or features—they buy self-respect, ease, confidence, security. They buy things that live in their heads, not the physical world. That's why, today, some of the most interesting management discussions revolve around business psychology and consumer behavior. Leaders who understand human emotions, who can empathize with what's going on beneath the surface, are more valuable than those who can just churn out products.

Take a hard look at what you're selling. Food? No—you're selling comfort, nostalgia, health. Banking? Wrong again. No one's buying a loan or a payment service; they're buying your support, your convenience. At the core, they're buying safety and progress in their own lives.

So here's a business priority for you: Figure out what's really being bought. Dig deep into the feeling that drives every transaction. Once you know that, reverse engineer your product or service to match it—so you're selling what's truly being purchased.

You don't sell engine capacity, acceleration stats, and fuel efficiency to someone whose fundamental feelings about a car have little to do with the car per se, but everything to do with where they are in their lives.

You don't sell RAM memory, megapixels, and processor speeds to the regular smartphone buyer. That works with the geeks, but the ordinary Joes and Janes may be looking for a signature device that says something about them, that is easy to use, and that becomes central to their everyday lives. What might cause them to buy? Stories that point out exactly how the device is going to improve their personal and family lives.

We all need to know this. What are our customers actually buying—which set of feelings? And then we need to start selling those feelings, by rethinking the CX journeys we deliver. Every point in the customer journey is a chance to evoke good feelings in our customers. When we focus on efficiency alone, we miss the opportunity to sell—and bank—feelings.

THE COMPLAINING CUSTOMER

Where there are people, there will be complaints.

The oldest recorded customer complaint dates back nearly four millennia, etched onto a clay tablet now housed in the British Museum. This ancient grievance, sent from Nanni to Ea-Nasir, a copper merchant in the Mesopotamian city of Ur, expressed frustration over the poor quality of copper ingots Nanni received in exchange for his silver.

Complaints are universal and inevitable, transcending time, geography, and technology. People complain in all epochs, in all languages, and using all media. As long as people buy things, they'll expect value and fairness—and, inevitably, those expectations won't always be met. Yet complaints remain what we dread most. Conditioned to avoid conflict, we often find it unpleasant to face disappointed customers and acknowledge where we fall short.

My father taught me a lifelong lesson at a young age: Cherish the complaining customer! Because that's a lifetime customer in disguise . . . provided you know what you're doing when folks complain.

Why do so many companies still not know how to handle complaining customers? Why do we keep failing such an elementary business test?

Picture this: A customer has a complaint, for whatever reason. They've reached out—maybe in person, or maybe via email, a tweet, a Facebook post, whatever. Now, here's how too many businesses respond.

- Step 1, *ignore* it. Pretend it never happened. Don't reply. Don't engage. Let the customer give up and disappear. After all, there are more customers where that one came from, right?
- If ignoring doesn't work, move to step 2: *Deny.* Refuse to accept fault. Throw the customer back at the page that has your terms and conditions. Subtly suggest the problem is probably on their end.
- If that doesn't silence them, there's step 3: *Argue.* Debate the complaint, go back and forth endlessly. Show them that you're no fool, and hint that maybe they're out to rip you off.
- And then there's step 4, the grand finale: *Insult.* Yell, call names, tell them where to go, maybe even call security. You laugh, but this happens more often than we think.

I hope you've never hit step 4, but I'd bet you've toyed with responses 1 through 3 more often than you'd like to admit. Let me quietly point out: Steps 1 through 3 are just as idiotic as step 4.

Why do we behave like this? We seem to forget that the point of a business is to have happy repeat customers. Too many of us see customers as an inconvenience to the smooth running of operations. We think business would be a breeze if only these annoying people would stop complaining.

Wrong. If your customers are constantly complaining, it means you're failing. You haven't created a product or experience that holds real value. You're on a sinking ship—it's just a question of when the final plunge happens.

Customer satisfaction is the ultimate measure of business success. Not revenue, not profits, not shareholder returns. Those metrics might look good in the short term, but they'll wither if your customer proposition is a sham.

Once you truly understand that, you'll put all your energy—and your team's—into making customers happy and fixing their problems, fast and fairly.

So here's how a smart business handles complaints.

- First: *Apologize.* Say you're sorry, whether it's technically your fault or not. If your customer feels let down—acknowledge that.
- Second: *Address* the issue. Look into what happened, and if you've wronged the customer, own it. Fix it. Replace the product, offer compensation—do more than just talk.
- Third: *Learn* from it. Dig into why things went wrong, identify recurring issues, and fix the root causes. It could be your people, your processes, or your systems—whatever it is, deal with it. Prevent it from

> happening again. Introduce long-term fixes, not just bandages.

The "ignore-deny-argue-insult" sequence? That's foolish. The "apologize-address-learn" approach? That's for those who understand what real business success looks like. So which path does your business follow?

This book has pointed out repeatedly: Real, lasting success comes from intangibles—the emotional connection you build with customers. They need to trust you to help them, not just sell to them. The first sequence destroys that trust, reducing your relationship to mere transactions. And when that happens, customers will drop you the second a better option appears.

Think about that next time a complaint pings somewhere in your universe. How are you about to respond? Through inaction, denial, argument, even abuse? Or will you be contrite, offer redress, and fix things for the future?

The second sequence is what transforms the complaining customer into the lifetime customer. When we complain, we are typically not ready to leave or do anything drastic. We are just expressing dissatisfaction in the hope of getting someone's attention. If that attention comes, and it is sincere, empathetic, and thoughtful? Hey, we're all in. Why wouldn't we be?

ARE YOU A GOOD CUSTOMER?

Let's flip the script to close this chapter.

Put your customer at the center of everything, and it'll pay off. That much we all know. But here's a question for you that you may not have thought about: Are you a good customer?

You might be scratching your head at that. I can almost hear the response: "What do you mean? I'm a customer! That's all there is to it. I'm always right; they're supposed to cater to me. My money keeps their lights on and their staff employed. They should be rolling out the red carpet, right?"

Sure, there's plenty of truth in that. As I tell every business I advise: Excellent customer service is non-negotiable if you want to survive in the long run. But here's the thing—just because you're the customer doesn't mean you get a free pass on decency.

After years of observing businesses in action, I can tell you this: Not all customers are equal. Most are great—they treat the relationship with respect, are polite, and play their part. They deserve the best service a business can offer. But there's a minority—a small yet toxic group. And they come in two flavors: egomaniacs and fraudsters.

The egomaniacs? They think being a customer gives them the right to be insufferable. They throw tantrums over the smallest hiccup, belittling staff and demanding personal apologies from CEOs for every minor slip-up. Some even launch public smear campaigns against businesses that make honest mistakes.

And then you've got the fraudsters, the ones who are out to exploit your business, sniffing out mistakes just so they can claim compensation or—worse—plotting elaborate scams while hiding under the "customer" halo. These folks? You need to show them the door, pronto.

Talk to any frontline employee, and they'll tell you that this bad bunch—though small—eats up an obscene amount of time and energy. Hours are wasted calming down egos, responding to wild claims, and soothing outrage that's often overblown. And because the mantra of "customer is king" has been drilled into businesses, these employees often feel unsupported when a difficult customer starts making noise.

Let's get real here: Being a customer entitles you to fair service, sure. It means you deserve a product that works and a quick, friendly response when things go wrong. But it does not entitle you to act like a jerk.

Relationships are a two-way street. If you want warm, friendly service, be warm and friendly. Don't like being treated rudely? Well, don't dish it out. Just because you're in a position of power—whether you're the buyer or the seller—doesn't mean you can throw basic decency out the window.

The best service providers are pleasant, no matter their market position. The best customers are respectful, no matter their buying power. On both sides, the top players are those who know how to be humble, gracious, and forgiving. A jerk—on either side—only makes everything harder.

I'm not asking you to put up with terrible service. But put things in perspective. Is this the first time the company has let you down? Forgive and move on. Assume they mean well—mistakes happen. Are they genuinely trying to make things right? Be patient, give them a chance. If the service remains poor, sure, take your business elsewhere. But hurling insults and creating drama? That's just you being a boor.

Relationships are a two-way street. If you want warm, friendly service, be warm and friendly.

And if you're the one delivering service, don't relax just because I've said some customers can be difficult. Keep doing your absolute best with every customer. Apologize quickly when things go wrong, offer redress without a fight, and learn from your mistakes. That's still the winning formula. Don't let a few bad apples make you forget the bigger picture: Providing a great customer experience is your best bet for long-term success.

In Closing

Don't compromise yourself. You're all you've got.

—Janis Joplin

Have you ever come across a restaurant that says things like this about its own menu?

"This one's not *that* good."

"This one's *not* authentic . . ."

"I'm surprised some people still order this."

Believe it or not, those are real descriptions from Aunt Dai, a Chinese restaurant in Montreal. The owner, Feigang Fei, writes brutally honest commentary about his food right on the menu. You'd think that approach would spell disaster for a restaurant, right? Wrong. His menu went viral in 2021. Customers started sharing the descriptions on social media, and suddenly, everyone wanted to try the food—not because they thought it was the best, but because they wanted to see if it really wasn't that good. Even Harvard's Schlesinger Library reportedly archived the menu.

Now, you might think this is some kind of clever PR stunt. But Fei comes across as genuinely sincere—a guy just calling it like it is. "A lot of people want to be the best," he said, "and we are simply not the best. We just try to be a little bit better every day." And that's what I love about this story. In a world full of BS, the person who tells the truth stands out.

I don't think Fei set out to be internet famous. He was just being himself, right there on the menu. A blogger happened to see it, tweeted it, and bam—instant fame. But why did it blow up? Simple: It's rare. In today's world, everyone's been taught to polish their image, pretend to be the best, and never admit anything is less than perfect. But let's be real—things usually aren't perfect, and pretending they are doesn't make them so.

Fei seems to simply be a man comfortable with the truth, striving to improve his business one honest step at a time. He just wanted to be transparent with his customers about his menu items, warning them about overly greasy or too-spicy dishes so they wouldn't end up ordering something they didn't want. It's a great reminder that in a world of constant image management, sometimes what people really crave is a little honesty.

We're conditioned to act like all our products are market-leading, like every workplace is world-class, and like our personal lives are some endless Instagram reel of excitement. But we know the truth: Most products are mediocre, most workplaces are tedious, and most lives are filled with the same old routine. Pretending otherwise doesn't fix anything.

We become better when we stop pretending there's nothing wrong. Real growth comes from acknowledging our flaws and working on them. I've met some of the best chefs—and they're never satisfied with their dishes. The best leaders? They talk openly about their own mistakes, not just other people's.

Let's not pretend to be what we're not. Let's be sincere in our promises, genuine in our attempts.

Look, everyone messes up. The great CEOs? They screw up daily. The biggest companies? They've got failed projects hidden away. The most respected leaders? They make bad calls all the time. Great relationships? Full of missteps. It's human nature to get things wrong. But covering it up with fake perfection only delays the inevitable. The truth always comes out, and no amount of flowery words or glossy branding will hide that.

We get better by facing what's wrong. We improve by admitting we're not the best—yet. Whether you're a chef, a leader, or just a human being, the path to genuine excellence isn't through pretending. It's through putting in the work and getting a little better, every single day. You don't fake it until you make it. You just keep making it better, and soon no fakery will be needed.

We should apply that lesson across our CX. Let's not pretend to be what we're not. Let's be sincere in our promises, genuine in our attempts. We don't win by talking ourselves up better than our competitors do; we win by actually striving to be better. Step 1 in that journey is to face up to what we actually are, and start improving from there.

DON'T DO FRU-FRU

Feigang Fei is an outlier, though.

My wife has a phrase she often uses to sum up the essence of many things: "just fru-fru."

What exactly is fru-fru? It's derived from "frou-frou" in the original French, and it refers to the surface-level frills that hide an empty core. It's the stuff that looks grand on the outside but lacks substance. Fru-fru is for the smooth talkers who can spin words beautifully but trip when it's time to deliver. It's the promises of the moon, only for you to end up with dust.

Once you spot it, fru-fru is everywhere.

It's especially rampant in corporate ranks. The sharp suits and sharper tongues rise, while the real workers are left in the background. These illusionists dazzle boardrooms and hiring committees with polished presentations and rehearsed charm. Meanwhile, the ones who get things done—who really deliver—are sidelined. And what gets sacrificed in all this? Quality—the thing that actually works.

And the rot trickles down. In today's companies, we see a flood of well-spoken, well-dressed customer reps who say all the right things, express over-the-top sympathy when you complain, and promise quick resolutions. But nothing changes. Problems persist, customers remain frustrated, and it's all smoothed over with sweet talk. The real work—building things that don't break, properly training staff—is neglected. Instead, the investment goes into fru-fru.

Modern media, both traditional and social, is a fru-fru playground. Talent and craft have been pushed aside in favor of clickbait and sensationalism. Fame today doesn't come from creating something of value; it's achieved by staying in the spotlight. Outlandish outfits, manufactured controversies, and empty platitudes are the tickets to stardom. Serious stories are drowned out by fluff, and we end up worshipping fru-fru celebrities with feet of clay.

Politicians? The maestros of fru-fru. Campaigns have become performances—full of promises that sparkle but rarely materialize. Elections dazzle with spectacle, yet real substance is scarce. Sadly, it works. Those with real plans and good intentions are often overshadowed by the crowd-pleasers who promise everything and deliver little. Fru-fru wins again.

Even in our personal lives, fru-fru sneaks in. The self-promoters, the witty talkers, those who dazzle with charm—they get all the attention. We seem to prefer shallow relationships in large numbers, rather than deeper, meaningful connections. The ones who are solid, loyal, and quiet? They're often ignored, even though they'd stand by you when it really matters. Glitter wins, even when there's no gold beneath.

So what do we do about this fru-fru pandemic, this quiet plague of our times? Honestly, not much right now. Fru-fru is spreading like a virus. But here's the thing: It eventually collapses under its own weight. You can only build so much on shaky foundations before the whole thing falls apart. Relationships, businesses, even nations built on fru-fru? They'll eventually crumble.

Real success comes from substance—products that work, solutions that last, and promises you can keep.

Sure, popularity might come from superficial glitz, but true progress comes from substance. Real accomplishments don't need loud marketing. Products need to work; solutions must solve problems. Leaders should deliver lasting results. Friends should be there when it counts.

When the froth of fru-fru finally fades—as it

always does—maybe then we'll see clearly again. We'll look for those who genuinely know their stuff. Leaders who've put in the work, who offer plans grounded in reality, not showmanship. Workers who take pride in a job well done, not just a good speech. Friends and partners who are there for you, not just in the good times but in the tough ones too.

But for that to happen, we—whether as voters, customers, or citizens—need to stop being dazzled by the fru-fru show. If something looks too good to be true, it probably is. We need to dig deeper, recognize illusions for what they are, and demand more.

Fru-fru is just decorative fluff—hollow, superficial, and fleeting. It's the empty flash that dazzles but leaves you wanting. Real success comes from substance—products that work, solutions that last, and promises you can keep.

Great CX, too, goes beyond fru-fru. It's not about looking good or talking well; it's about delivering. It's about meaning what you say and doing what you promise. Training people to be good, not just to look or sound good. Valuing real work over the appearance of work.

In the end, great CX doesn't need fru-fru. It's grounded, genuine, and committed to helping customers. And that's what really matters.

HOW TO GET GOING WITH GREAT CX

You've read most of the book. Now what are you going to do with it?

It's easy to feel fired up with inspiration and yet still not act. We're human, after all—life's full of distractions, emotions that get in the way, and surprises that knock us off track.

But I'm not letting you walk away without a practical, structured way to put the key lessons of this book into action. Let's break it down into short-term, medium-term, and long-term steps, using a simple, high-impact framework (based on something that Jerry Angrave offers in his book, *The Journey Mapping Playbook*). Here are my own recommended actions, based on decades of observation of CX that works:

In the short run, be tactical.

Drain the pain. You likely have plenty of CX issues to tackle—so get to it! Use the insights from chapters 3 and 6, and review your customer journeys. Where are you causing the most pain for your customers? Be brutally honest, and face the home truths. Your first CX goal: Eliminate the bad stuff you're doing. Human fixes, digital fixes—get them done.

Start saying sorry, and mean it. Nothing jump-starts a customer-centric culture like genuine apologies. Say it from the top, and get everyone else to follow. *Say* sorry so you don't have to keep *being* sorry. Avoid legal jargon and loopholes—just own up, and work hard to not repeat mistakes.

Insert little touches. You don't need a grand strategy to inject moments of wow. Encourage your team to be warmer, more human. Walk the floor, point out good CX, and call out the bad. Bring back the basics: *sorry*, *please*, and *thank you*. The small things add up.

Coach the coaches. One of the most effective ways to get cracking is to improve frontline supervision. Look out for your CX champions, those who interact beautifully with customers, those who are naturals. Give them the challenge of producing others like them—by walking around coaching and coaxing, correcting and clarifying. Keep it simple. You may be surprised at how things improve without that much effort.

In the medium run, be strategic.

Design human incentives. To drive great CX, don't rely on the tired carrot-and-stick approach. Make it personal. Show people how better CX helps them succeed, not just the company. Reward the right behavior on the spot—while it's fresh. And don't just throw money at people—give them ownership, pride, and purpose.

Do digital properly. Digital CX isn't about flashy apps or trendy AI; it's about using data smartly to really know your customers. You probably have a ton of information already—analyze it. Use AI to spot problems early and tailor experiences. But don't let tech take over—keep the human touch. Customers don't want to feel processed. Use digital tools to enhance, not replace, real interactions. It's about being smart with data but still treating both employees and customers like people, not algorithms.

Humanize the HR. You know this by now: The real CX strategy is a people strategy. Great CX is rooted in how you treat your employees. Hire people who care about doing things right, not just ticking boxes. Reward behaviors that lead to excellent customer outcomes—genuine care, attention to detail, going that extra mile. Your HR systems should reflect this, recognizing effort, not just numbers.

In the long run, be cultural.

Start with boundaries. Culture is the game changer, as we've stressed throughout. Once customer satisfaction is valued, the hardest part of leadership is done. But changing culture takes time. Start by setting clear boundaries: These behaviors (ignoring customers, arguing with them) will get you fired. Others (going out of your way to help, stepping in for colleagues) will get you promoted. Enforce it daily, and culture will adjust. Once people know it's serious, culture starts adjusting rapidly.

Set the tone from the top. If leaders want a better culture, they have to be that culture. They can't just talk about it—they must live it. Role modeling is the most powerful transmission mechanism in leadership. If the leaders show they care about CX, it will spread. No option here: If you want a customer-focused culture, you need leaders who embody it. People become their leaders over time. A culture that's hot on CX needs a leadership team that's even hotter on CX.

Embed the culture. CX becomes real when it's woven into everyday behavior. Make customer empathy a core value—something everyone practices, from the front lines to the deepest recesses of the back office. Regularly put yourself in the customer's shoes. Share CX feedback openly and act on it. Recognize and reward great CX daily—not just with bonuses, but with genuine appreciation. Culture becomes real when it becomes a natural, everyday state of being. Making a great CX culture part of the everyday routine means embedding it in everything you do—not treating it as an occasional project or a buzzword. Create rituals around CX—daily huddles, quick feedback loops, and sharing CX wins at team meetings.

Keep it simple, stupid. Most importantly, keep your CX culture straightforward. Overcomplicating things turns CX into a chore. Instead, build a routine where everyone contributes—whether they're solving problems, streamlining processes, or showing genuine care. When CX becomes second nature, that's when it sticks.

A FINAL WORD: DO GREAT CX—FOR YOU

Why is CX so important? It's because it helps the company make more money and employees earn more bonuses, right?

Yes—but only up to a point.

I want to end this book by pointing out that there's a deal bigger than that in play here. Do we just do this CX thing because it creates better financial rewards? What about doing it because it's actually a fine thing to be doing?

The final example in this book is about Sonya Kassam, who runs a microbusiness in Kenya, an online store called Ustawi. She is one of the most naturally customer-centered people I have ever known. She practically radiates joy when her customers call or message her to praise her warm service and quick delivery. Yes, she runs this business to provide for her family, but that's only part of the story. Sonya is genuinely invested in every customer she serves, committed to getting each order delivered without delay.

She cares about her customers because she cares about people.

To be kind to people is a sign of human nobility. Customers are just people who are dealing with you. They are seeking answers to their questions, solutions for their challenges, succor and ease in their lives. Can you not do that for them, not as an employee or a representative or an agent—but just as a good human?

When I watch an employee and a customer having a good interaction, I am always heartened. Not just because the CX on display is good, but because the *humanity* on display is good.

Delivering great CX isn't just about boosting the bottom line—it's about something much bigger. It's about human decency. When we go out of our way to help a customer, solve their problem, or just make their day a little better, we're expressing the best of what it means to be human. There's virtue and honor in serving others with care, respect, and empathy. It's not just a transaction; it's a connection. And that connection elevates us.

Yes, delivering excellent customer experiences will improve your business outcomes. Your customers will stay loyal, your reputation will grow, and your profits will rise. But the real reward isn't financial—it's human. When we take pride in being helpful, in going beyond what's expected, we grow as individuals. We tap into something deeper and more meaningful than just doing a job. We remind ourselves and others that life isn't just about getting through the day—it's about making someone else's day better.

In CX, as in everything else, we should aim to play bigger than ourselves. When we step outside our self-interest and focus on others—whether it's a customer, a colleague, or anyone else—we grow as people. Delivering great CX is just one expression of that bigger purpose. It's not just a business strategy; it's a way to become a better human being. And when we all strive to play that bigger game, we lift everyone around us.

Delivering great CX isn't just about boosting the bottom line—it's about something much bigger. It's about human decency.

In the end, being kind, helpful, and attentive to others is what truly elevates us. It's what makes the world better. The financial rewards are fine, but the human rewards—those moments when you know you've made a difference in someone's life—those will always outshine any bottom-line success. So let's not just focus on CX as a business tool. Let's see it for what it really is: an opportunity to be better humans, and to make the world a little kinder, one interaction at a time.

THANK YOU

For over two decades, I've shared my weekly thoughts in Kenya's *Sunday Nation*, and much of what I've learned about customer experience first took shape there. Many ideas in this book were born in those pages. I remain deeply grateful to the editors who've supported me along the way, showing unwavering enthusiasm for my work.

I also want to acknowledge the invaluable contributions of my team at Sunwords, and the extended family that powers Fast Forward, the leadership program I founded. Year after year, they show up energized and eager to deliver world-class customer experiences to each fresh cohort of leaders. In the beginning, they responded to my guidance on CX; today, they teach and inspire me on what it means to really deliver.

Finally, a special word for my wife, Shriti. This book is as much hers as it is mine. She brings me a daily stream of customer experiences—both good and bad—and often has the sharpest insights on what should be done about them. She's my first reader and first editor. The phrase "just fru-fru" is hers, and it taught me a vital lesson: there's no value in cloaking CX in fake frippery. It's always better to stay modest but real.

AUTHOR'S NOTE

Throughout this book, I've highlighted organizations and leaders that are doing exceptional things with customer experience. These examples were chosen carefully, based on their current excellence. But let me be clear: Nothing in CX remains fixed. What's outstanding today could stumble tomorrow. Great customer experience requires constant vigilance and effort—it's not a trophy you win and keep forever.

So while the examples here are worth learning from, this is not a blanket endorsement of any organization, person, or offering. Businesses must continue to evolve and adapt to the changing needs of their customers. Even the best can drop the ball if they lose sight of that. Stay on your toes, because in CX, the game is never over.

DIVE DEEPER, EXPLORE WIDER

» *The Journey Mapping Playbook*, by Jerry Angrave (De Gruyter, 2020)
» *The Effortless Experience*, by Matthew Dixon, Nick Toman, and Rick DeLisi (Penguin, 2013)
» *A New Way to Think*, by Roger Martin (Harvard Business Review Press, 2022)
» *The Customer Copernicus*, by Charlie Dawson and Seán Meehan (Routledge, 2021)
» *Working Backwards*, by Colin Bryar and Bill Carr (Pan Macmillan, 2022)
» *The Human Experience*, by John Sills (Bloomsbury, 2023)
» *Digital Darwinism*, by Tom Goodwin (Kogan Page, 2022)
» *Uncommon Service*, by Frances Frei and Anne Morriss (Harvard Business Review Press, 2012)
» *The Customer Service Revolution*, by John DiJulius (Greenleaf Book Group, 2015)

ABOUT THE AUTHOR

Sunny Bindra is a sense-maker, helping leaders and organizations thrive by cutting through complexity. As an advisor, writer, and speaker, he works closely with top CEOs and leadership teams, driving big-picture thinking and bold change. His clients have included banking giants, startups, and transformative public-sector projects. Whether guiding boards, coaching executives, or elevating customer experience, he unlocks innovation by seeing people, not just assets. He leads Fast Forward, a sought-after leadership program, and is a long-standing *Sunday Nation* columnist. This is his fifth book.

www.sunwords.com
@sunnysunwords
Sunwords by Sunny Bindra

www.ingramcontent.com/pod-product-compliance
Ingram Content Group UK Ltd.
Pitfield, Milton Keynes, MK11 3LW, UK
UKHW040311100625
459464UK00001B/10

9 789914 374469